REMEMBRANCE OF ALLAH

Zikr-i-Ilahi

A lecture delivered by Hadhrat Mirza Bashiruddin Mahmud Ahmad,
Khalifatul-Masih II (May Allah be pleased with him),
during the annual conference of
the Ahmadiyya Muslim Community on December 28, 1916.

Remembrance of Allah
(Originally published in Urdu as *Zikr-i-Ilahi*)
By: Hadhrat Mirza Bashiruddin Mahmud Ahmad
  Khalifatul-Masih II[ra]

Translated into English by: Munawar Ahmed Saeed
© Islam International Publications Ltd.
  First edition (UK) 1993
  Present edition (UK) 2003

Published by:
Islam International Publications Ltd.
Islamabad
Sheephatch Lane,
Tilford, Surrey, GU10 2AQ
United Kingdom
All rights reserved
Printed in the United Kingdom at :
Raqeem Press
Islamabad, Tilford, Surrey, GU10 2AQ

ISBN: 1 85372 509 9

Contents

Publisher's Note   v

Glossary of Important Terms   vii

The Abbreviations   xi

1. **Remembrance of Allah**   1
   What is Zikr-i-Ilahi or Remembrance of Allah?   1

2. **Importance of the Subject**   3
   Why is Zikr-i-Ilahi Necessary?   3
   Need of Greater Attention to Zikr in Our Community   5

3. **Misunderstandings about Zikr**   9
   Misguided Forms of Zikr   9
   Zikr vs. Mesmerism   11
   Pleasure from Zikr   11
   Difference Between Zikr and Mere Influence of Thoughts   12
   Reciting Zikr Aloud   13
   Poetry as Zikr?   13

4. **Characteristics of True Zikr According to Islamic Teachings**   15
   True Zikr Rules Out Dancing and Shouting   16
   Unconsciousness is Not a Proper Result of Zikr   16
   Four Kinds of Zikr Enjoined by Islam   18

5   **Methods of Performing Zikr**   21
    Recitation of the Holy Qur'an   21
    Expressing the Greatness and Glory of Allah and Thanking Him   22
    Proclaiming Unity of Allah as Zikr   24
    Other Recitations   24

6   **Precautions and Proper Times for this Form of Zikr**   27
    Necessary Precautions for Zikr   27
    Proper Times for Zikr   30

7   **The Prayers**   33
    The Philosophy of Prescribing Sunnah and Nawafil   33
    How to Get Up at Night for Tahajjud   34
    Concentrating in Prayers   40

8   **Public Proclamation as Remembrance**   55
    Benefits of Zikr   56

References of the Holy Qur'an   63

Index   65

REMEMBRANCE OF ALLAH

Publisher's Note

Alhamdolillah, "All Praise belongs to Allah" who has enabled us to prepare this second edition of the English rendering of a speech delivered by Hadhrat Musleh Mau'ood Mirza Bashiruddin Mahmud Ahmad, Khalifatul-Masih II (*radiyallahu anhu*) on December 28, 1916. The translation is based on the Urdu text of *Zikr-i-Ilahi* printed by Fazl-e-Umar Foundation (Rabwah, December 1982).

The revered speaker was the Promised Son of the Holy Founder of the Ahmadiyya Muslim Community, Hadhrat Mirza Ghulam Ahmad, the Promised Messiah (*alaihissalam*) (1835–1908). In 1914, at the age of 25, he was elected as *Khalifa*, that is, successor, to the Promised Messiah[as]. For 52 years he led the Community and served the causes for which it was established. He inspired and motivated his followers' spiritual development; he spoke and wrote in defense of Islam; and he established institutions to propagate Islam all over the world.

Remebrance of Allah (*Zikr-i-Ilahi*) shows a true understanding of the relationship between Allah, the Creator, and the human beings in search of Him. It is replete with points of wisdom on how that relationship can be nurtured through the remembrance of Allah. It is a treasure that will benefit all those who use it to inculcate a living relationship with their Creator. We pray that this book becomes a source of promoting a true understanding about Allah and helping many to attain His love and nearness.

The publisher would like to acknowledge with thanks the help of Mr. Munawar A. Saeed, and his children, Uzma Saeed Ahmad and Ahmed Muneeb Saeed in preparing the original translation and this revised version. For improving the format of this second edition we are grateful to Abdul-Wahab Mirza, who received valuable assistance from Jaleel Ahmad Akbar, Muhammad Dawood Khokhar, Salman Sajid, Syed Sajid Ahmad and Tariq Amjad. Allah reward them all.

All Praise belongs to Allah, Lord of all the worlds.

The Publishers
Islam International Publications Ltd.
Islamabad
Sheephatch Lane,
Tilford, Surrey
GU10 2AQ
United Kingdom
July 2003

Glossary of Important Terms

For the benefit of readers, some important Islamic terms are explained below.

Allah. Allah is the personal name of God in Islam. To show proper reverence for Him, the Muslims often add *Ta'ala*, the Most High, when saying His Holy name.

Adhan. Call for formal Islamic Prayer.

Ahmadiyya Muslim Community. Community of Muslims who have accepted the claims of Hadhrat Mirza Ghulam Ahmad[as] of Qadian as the Promised Messiah. The Community was established by the Promised Messiah[as] in 1889, and is now under the leadership of his fifth *Khalifa*, Hadhrat Mirza Masroor Ahmad (may Allah strengthen him). The Community is also known as Jama'at Ahmadiyya. A member of the Community is called an Ahmadi Muslim or an Ahmadi.

Aleem. An attribute of Allah, which means the All Knowing.

Annual Conference. A conference held annually and attended by Ahmadi and non-Ahmadi Muslims and other people throughout the world in large numbers. The annual conference was initiated by the Promised Messiah[as] in 1891. It is known by its original Urdu name, *Jalsa Salana*.

Hadith. Saying of the Holy Prophet Muhammad *(sallallahu alaihi wa sallam)*

Hadhrat. A term of respect used for a person of established righteousness and piety.

Hadhur. Your Honor/Holiness, His Honor/Holiness.

Holy Prophet[saw]. A term used exclusively for Hadhrat Muhammad, the Holy Prophet of Islam (peace and blessings of Allah be upon him).

Holy Qur'an. The book sent by Allah for the guidance of all mankind. It was revealed to the Holy Prophet (peace and blessings of Allah be upon Him), over a period of twenty-three years.

Khabeer. An attribute of Allah, which means the All Aware.

Khalifa. Caliph is derived from the Arabic word *Khalifa*, which herein means the successor. In Islamic terminology, the word righteous *Khalifa* is applied to one of the four *Khalifas* who continued the mission of Muhammad[saw], the Holy Prophet of Islam. Ahmadi Muslims refer to a successor of the Promised Messiah[as] as *Khalifatul-Masih*.

Khaliq. An attribute of Allah, which means the Creator.

Musleh Mau'ood. A term, meaning Promised Reformer, applied to Hadhrat Khalifatul-Masih II, Mirza Bashiruddin Mahmud Ahmad[ra]. He is called *Musleh Mau'ood* because he was born in accordance with a prophecy made by the Promised Messiah[as] in 1886 about the birth of a righteous son who would be endowed with special abilities, attributes and powers. The life and works of Hadhrat Mirza Bashiruddin Mahmud Ahmad[ra] are a testimony to the fulfillment of the prophecy.

Prayer and Prayers. Three Islamic terms, all sometimes translated as prayer, should be distinguished.

The first term is *Du'aa* or supplications made of God Almighty. *Du'aa* can be made at any time and in any language. It does not require any formal prescribed posture. *Du'aa* is translated in the text as 'prayer'.

Secondly, *Salat* refers to the five daily Prayer services prescribed for all Muslims. Unlike *Du'aa*, *Salat* has fixed timings and modes of performance. We have retained the term *Salat* in the translation or have used the term 'prescribed Prayer', or 'Prayer'. Each Prayer is divided into *Rak'a*. Each *Rak'as* includes several postures—standing *Qiyam*, bowing *Ruku*, sitting *Qa'adah*, and prostration *Sajdah*. The prescribed Prayers have three components:

Fard, those enjoined by Allah; *Sunnah*, those offered regularly by the Holy Prophet[saw] and enjoined by him; and *Nafl*, the voluntary components (discussed below).

Nafl means to do more than is required by duty or obligation i.e. voluntary. *Nawafil* is the plural of *Nafl*. *Nawafil*, which are similar in form to *Salat*, may be offered independently or in conjunction with a prescribed Prayer. Performance of *Nawafil*, though not obligatory, is highly meritorious. One *Nafl* Prayer of great merit is *Tahajjud*, the late night Prayer.

Promised Messiah. This term refers to the founder of the Ahmadiyya Muslim Community, Hadhrat Mirza Ghulam Ahmad[as] of Qadian. He claimed that he had been sent by Allah in accordance with prophecies of the Holy Prophet[saw] about the coming, in latter days of a *Mahdi* (the Guided One) and Messiah from among the Muslims.

Tasbeeh. Glorification of Allah by reciting *SubhanAllah* (Holy is Allah), or other phrases.

Tahmeed. Expressing thanks to Allah by reciting *Alhamdolillah* (All Praise belongs to Allah).

Takbeer. Proclaiming the Greatness of Allah by reciting, *AllahoAkbar* (Allah is the Greatest).

Tirmidhi. A book which contains collections of *Hadiths*.

Qadir. An attribute of Allah, which means the All Powerful.

Quddoos. An attribute of Allah, which means the Holy.

Zakat. Prescribed alms.

Zikr and Zikr-i-Ilahi *Zikr* is an Arabic word meaning remembrance. *Zikr-i-Ilahi* means the remembrance of Allah.

The Abbreviations

The following abbreviations have been used. Readers are requested to recite the full salutations when reading the book:

SAW. An abbreviation for *Sallallahu Alaihi Wa Sallam*, meaning "May the blessings of Allah and peace be upon him," is written after the name of the Holy Prophet[saw].

AS. An abbreviation *Alaihissalam*, meaning "Peace be upon him" is written after the name of prophets other than the Holy Prophet[saw].

RA. An abbreviation *Radiyallahu Anhu* and *Radiyallahu Anha*, meaning, "May Allah be pleased with him" and "May Allah be pleased with her" is written after the names of the Companions of the Holy Prophet[saw] and of the Promised Messiah[as].

ABOUT THE AUTHOR

Hadhrat Musleh Mau'ood, Mirza Bashir-ud-Din Mahmud Ahmad[ra] was the Promised Son and the second *Khalifa* of the Promised Messiah[as], the Holy Founder of the Ahmadiyya Muslim Community. Born in accordance with a mighty prophecy of the Promised Messiah[as], he was gifted with knowledge, both secular and divine. His understanding of the Holy Qur'an and Islmaic matters was immense. He wrote a detailed commentary covering several chapters of the Holy Qur'an. His books and lectures are replete with points of wisdom and understanding. He was the prince of exposition—both in writing and speech. He was filled with the light Divine.

In 1914, at the age of 25, he was elected as *Khalifa*, that is, successor, to the Promised Messiah[as]. For 52 years he led the Community and served the causes for which it was established. He inspired and motivated his followers' sprirtual development; he spoke and wrote in defense of Islam; and he established institutions to propagate Islam all over the world.

بِسْمِ اللهِ الرَّحْمٰنِ الرَّحِيْمِ

REMEMBRANCE OF ALLAH
(Zikr-i-Ilahi)

After reciting the creed of Islam and seeking the protection of Allah, Hadhur said:
I wish to address the following matters:
- What is *Zikr-i-Ilahi*, or Remembrance of Allah?
- Why is *Zikr-i-Ilahi* necessary?
- The various forms of *Zikr-i-Ilahi*.
- Precautions to be taken in performing *Zikr-i-Ilahi*.
- Common misconceptions about *Zikr-i-Ilahi*.
- Methods of eradicating Satanic influences and maintaining concentration in Prayer.

This subject is of uiversal importance. It concerns all human beings—the high and the low, the rich and the poor, the young and the old. If you hear something from me which appears insignificant to you, do not ignore it; when you put these ideas in practice, you will be convinced that it was not insignificant, but was the bearer of magnificent beneficial results.

What is Zikr-i-Ilahi, or Remembrance of Allah?

Zikr, an Arabic word, means remembrance. When used for Allah, it refers to the ways of remembering Allah: Keeping His attributes in mind, reciting them again and again, affirming them with eagerness and sincerity, and reflecting upon His Omnipotence and Power.

Importance of the Subject

How important is *Zikr-i-Ilahi*? To put it briefly, it is vital and of great importance. I do not call it great simply as a manner of speech, but because of Allah Himself has called it so. Allah the Most High says in the Holy Qur'an:

$$...وَلَذِكْرُ اللّٰهِ اَكْبَرُ...$$

...and remembrance of Allah indeed is the greatest virtue... (29:46)

That is, remembrance of Allah is higher in status than all other acts of worship. The statement that this subject is vital and important is therefore not mine; it is a pronouncement of Allah Himself.

Why is Zikr-i-Ilahi Necessary?

If the subject is of such great importance, Islam would obviously place constant emphasis upon it. This is indeed the case. We find frequent reminders about it in the Holy Qur'an, for example,

$$وَاذْكُرِ اسْمَ رَبِّكَ بُكْرَةً وَّاَصِيْلًا$$

And remember the name of thy Lord during the morning as well as the evening. (76:26)

Similarly there is a Hadith in which the Holy Prophet (*sallallahu alaihi wa sallam*) says, when people gather together for the remembrance of Allah they are surrounded by angels and are covered by mercy from their Lord.

This is why I have selected this subject for the annual conference. Thousands of you have come from great distances to attend this gathering. When I speak on this subject, the angels will shower Allah's Bless-

Why is Zikr-i-Ilahi Necessary?

ings upon all of you. When you return home and repeat what you have heard, your listeners will receive the blessings. Thus, the blessings will be widely shared by the whole Community…

The Hadith which I mentioned earlier shows that remembrance of Allah in a gathering is a blessed event. It attracts angels who bring with them the blessings and mercy of Allah. The importance of *Zikr* should, therefore, be evident. Obviously, the angels will honor a person who, by performing *Zikr,* attracts their company often. The more time he spends in the remembrance of Allah, the more will he attract the company of angels and they will constantly remind him to perform good deeds.

The existence of angels is not a fabrication of human imagination; it is a certainty. I myself have seen angels. I once conversed with them in a very informal manner. Through their frequent visits, angels cultivate friendship and affinity with those who remember Allah.

Then God Almighty says:

$$\text{يَٰٓأَيُّهَا الَّذِينَ اٰمَنُوْا لَا تُلْهِكُمْ اَمْوَالُكُمْ وَلَا اَوْلَادُكُمْ عَنْ ذِكْرِ اللّٰهِ ...}$$

O ye who believe let not your wealth and your children divert you from the remembrance of Allah… (63:10)

$$\text{يَٰٓأَيُّهَا الَّذِينَ اٰمَنُوا اذْكُرُوا اللّٰهَ ذِكْرًا كَثِيْرًا * وَّسَبِّحُوْهُ بُكْرَةً وَّ اَصِيْلًا *}$$

O ye who believe, remember Allah much. And glorify Him morning and evening. (33:42–43)

The Holy Prophet[saw] has stressed the importance of *Zikr* in his Hadith. Hadhrat Abu Musa Ash'ari[ra] relates that the Holy Prophet[saw] said, "The comparison between a person who remembers his Lord and the one who does nto do so, is like that of the living and the dead." That is, he who remembers Allah is alive he, who does not, is dead. This clearly shows how important remembrance of Allah is.

There is another Hadith reported in *Tirmidhi*. Hadhrat Abi Dardaa[ra] relates, that when the Holy Prophet[saw] addressed his Companions, he said, "Shall I tell you about your best action and the noblest deed (even for the kings) which raises your status, is better for you than spending gold and silver, and better for you than that you meet your enemy and cut off their necks, or that you yourselves attain martyrdom?" The Companions said, *"Certainly, please tell us."* The Holy Prophet[saw] said, "It is the remembrance of Allah."

According to another Hadith the Holy Prophet[saw] said, "Remembrance of Allah has a great reward." A Companion asked, "O Prophet of Allah, is it higher in reward than striving in the cause of Allah?" He said, *"Yes, because it is the remembrance of Allah which encourages you to undertake the striving."*

Need of Greater Attention to Zikr in Our Community

Such is the importance and necessity of *Zikr*. Yet, in some respects, many members of our Community do not pay due attention to it. God Almighty has naturally inclined me to reflect and ponder. I have pondered over this matter ever since my adolescence and I am equally concerned now as I was then. Any laxity in the remembrance of Allah, which exists in our Community, must be removed.

The Promised Messiah (*alaihissalam*) has laid great emphasis on Prayer. By the Grace of God, our Community is very mindful of this obligation. The Promised Messiah[as] has also stressed the importance of remembrance of Allah, but the Community has not yet given it the required attention.

Laxity in the remembrance of Allah results, in part, from the influence of Western education. Many people think that there is no point in sitting alone and saying *La Ilaha Illallah* (There is none worthy of worship except Allah) or reciting the attributes of God like *Quddoos* (the Holy), *Aleem* (the All Knowing), *Khabeer* (the All Aware), *Qadir* (the All Powerful), or *Khaliq* (the Creator). Many of our members have been exposed to Western education, and have therefore been influenced by these ideas. Farmers constitute another large group in our Community. In the past, they have not been well informed about the concept of *Zikr* and its benefit. Hence, they also lack the habit of *Zikr*. Unless the farming community is adequately informed and properly instructed, it cannot be expected to pay sufficient regard to the remembrance of Allah.

Need of Greater Attention to Zikr in Our Community

Salat (performance of the five prescribed Prayers during the day) is also remembrance of Allah. By the Grace of Allah our Community is very regular in observing *Salat*. However, there are important methods of remembering Allah other than *Salat*. Although they are not totally lacking in the Community, adequate attention is not being paid to them and some members do not put them in practice. This is a major flaw. Listen! If someone is exceptionally handsome but has deformed eyes, ears or nose, will he be called handsome? Not at all! Everybody will say that he is repulsive. In other words, a member who does not employ some methods of remembering Allah is like a person who is wearing a very expensive coat, shirt, jacket and trousers, but lacks shoes or head-dress. Despite his well-tailored clothes, his missing shoes or head-dress makes his appearance defective. Absence of the habit of remembering Allah is a defect, and people with good taste dislike any personal defect.

I will demonstrate that in addition to *Salat*, ways of remembering Allah have been prescribed by Allah and His Messenger. Whether one fully comprehends the philosophy of these commandments or not, it is essential to follow them to attain spiritual excellence.

Some members of our Community imagine that by performing obligatory worship they have done their duty and there is no need for *Nawafil* (the voluntary Prayers). This is a misconception. The Holy Prophet[saw] says that God Almighty told him, "By offering *Nawafil* My servant gets so close to Me that I become the ears with which he hears, the eyes with which he sees, the hands with which he holds, and the feet with which he walks." This Hadith reveals the value given to *Nawafil* by Allah, and the high status of a person who performs them. Allah elevates him so high that he begins to absorb His attributes. Therefore, *Nawafil* are not an ordinary matter. It is a cause for great concern that many people pay no attention to them.

Man is prone to laxity and indolence. He wishes to cope with the minimum of hardship and discipline. God Almighty, Who knows the weaknesses of His creatures, has, by His grace, appointed some acts of worship as obligatory and others as voluntary. The obligatory worship sets the acceptable standard; anyone who meets it fully will be above reproach. It is narrated that a person came to the Holy Prophet[saw] and asked about Islam. He responded, "Five Prayers during the day and night." He asked, "Any Prayer other than these?" The Holy Prophet[saw] said, "None, unless you yourself desire." Then the Holy Prophet^{saw} continued, "Fasting during the month of Ramadan." Again the man asked, "Any fasts other than these?" The Holy Prophet^{saw} responded, "None, unless you yourself desire." Then the Holy Prophet^{saw} told him about *Zakat*, the financial obligation of the Muslims. He repeated the same question and received the similar reply. The man left saying, "I promise in the name of Allah that I shall not add anything to these, nor shall I miss any of them." The Holy Prophet^{saw} said, "If he speaks the truth, he has attained success."

Need of Greater Attention to Zikr in Our Community

In short, obligatory worship, performed perfectly, assures success. But the careful and the wise do not restrict themselves to obligatory worship. They enter the field of *Nawafil* to make up for possible shortcomings in their observance of obligatory worship. For instance, five daily Prayers have been prescribed. However, a lapse or omission may have occurred during some of them, rendering them useless. There will be an obligation owed on the Day of Judgement for all such shortcomings in Prayers. *Nawafil* will compensate for such an obligation.

It is narrated that the Holy Prophet^{saw} once saw one of his Companions observing Prayer. He asked him to repeat his Prayer, which he did. But the Holy Prophet^{saw} asked him to repeat for the second, and then for a third time. The Companion pleaded, "O Prophet of Allah, I do not know how to pray better; please teach me." The Holy Prophet^{saw} responded, "You were rushing with your Prayer and therefore it is not worthy of acceptance by Allah. Pray slowly and it will be accepted."

Let me illustrate this point. Suppose a student takes an examination in which he requires fifty marks to pass. If he answers questions worth only fifty marks, he cannot be sure of his success. He may fail because one of the questions may have been answered wrong. Or imagine a traveler about to undertake a long journey. He may estimate the money required during his journey, but during the travel he may be faced with emergency requiring additional funds. *Nawafil* are like the extra funds for emergencies. They are important and should receive particular attention..

Misunderstandings about Zikr

There is a common misunderstanding about *Zikr* in our Community. Since it appears to result in neglect of *Zikr*, I want to remove this misunderstanding. The Promised Messiah[as] criticized the *Sufis* (the so-called devotees) of his time who have introduced many innovations in Islam. He pointed out that their repeating, parrot-fashion, of different phrases of *Zikr* was useless; it was time to defend Islam from the attacks of the enemies. The Promised Messiah[as] criticized them—and this they indeed deserved—but some Ahmadis have misunderstood him. The conclusion that sitting at a place in remembrance of Allah has no merit is absolutely wrong.

All forms of *Zikr* are meant to praise Allah and to glorify His Name. The Promised Messiah[as] criticized those who verbalized the Glory of God in the privacy of their homes, but did not challenge the enemies heaping affront upon His Holy Name. He admonished them because they were indolent. They were not performing their duty of calling people towards goodness and forbidding them from evil. Their actions amounted to hypocrisy. If they were sincere in their glorification of God, why did they not counter the attacks of the enemies? Why did they not glorify Allah on the public platform as they did in the quiet corners of their homes?

Moreover, the Promised Messiah[as] criticized them because they defaced the concept of *Zikr*. Their practices had no trace of the concept of remembrance of God in its pristine purity.

Misguided Forms of Zikr

Several misguided forms of *Zikr* are found among the *Sufis*. They utter a cry from their hearts and take it to their heads and shout so loudly that nobody in the vicinity can sleep or concentrate on worship. This is called

Misguided Forms of Zikr penetrating the heart—as if *La Ilaha Illallah* would enter their hearts only if it was hammered in! Although they say that they are gathering for *Zikr,* they only delude themselves with empty sounds of "Allah, Allah."

There are many practices:

- Some simply have a good time with songs, choruses and dancing by call girls; they call it a meeting of *Zikr,* because the sound of Allah is frequently made.
- Some penetrate their hearts.
- Some utter a cry from their soul.
- Some raise *Zikr* from their hearts and it returns after performing a prostration at Arsh—the Throne of Allah.
- Some utter cries of Allah from every particle of their body.
- Some dance to the sound of the verses of the Holy Qur'an with others hopping around and reciting poetry. They feign intoxication and unconsciousness. Someone then jumps into the middle of the gathering with shrill shrieks of "Allah, Allah."

In short, many eccentric and occult practices have been introduced into the concept of *Zikr;* none of them has anything to do with the true teachings of Islam. We condemn these innovations, but we cannot forsake *Zikr* because of them.

The Holy Prophet[saw] has said, "Every innovation takes one away from the right path and all of them lead to fire. That is why such *Zikr* does not lead these people closer to Allah; instead, it moves them away from Him."

Ever since this type of *Zikr* has been introduced, Muslims have drifted away from Allah. This is not surprising: practices contrary to the directions of Allah and His Apostle were bound to weaken spiritually.

All innovations introduced into *Zikr* have an element of pleasure, but the pleasure is artificial. The man who succumbs to it at the cost of real pleasure is ruined. He is like someone who suffers from stomach ache and, rather than seeking proper treatment, goes to sleep with a dose of opium. The narcotic effect provides a temporary relief, but in fact he is killing himself. A time will soon come when his disease will do its damage.

Zikr vs. Mesmerism

What is called *Zikr* by these people is actually mesmerism and hypnotism. It has nothing to do with spirituality; rather, it is related to concentration of thoughts.

God Almighty has vested the human mind with the power to produce a very strong influence by focused thoughts. Feelings of pleasure—similar to those derived from opium, cocaine, or marijuana—can be derived from such concentration. These sensations are not real pleasure, but a state of numbness. Such people fool themselves into believing that they receive pleasure by reciting the name of Allah. Actually, even if they said *Ram* at that time their feelings would be no different.

It is narrated that a respected Muslim was traveling in a boat. He started his *Zikr* with full concentration. Others, mainly Hindus in the boat, joined him in saying "Allah, Allah." However, a Hindu ascetic was not influenced. The Muslim focused his thoughts upon the ascetic, who, in turn, started focusing upon the Muslim with greater force. Instead of influencing the ascetic, the Muslim was influenced himself. Quite involuntarily, he started saying "Ram, Ram." The Muslim was astonished and realized that performing *Zikr* in this manner was futile. He repented and stopped his practice. He recognized that the result was merely produced by the exercise of a skill, and not by the remembrance of Allah. If the blessing of saying Allah was the source of his comfort, uttering "Ram" could not have created the same feelings.

Those who perform such rituals are like a traveler famishing in a desert. Finding a bag filled with pebbles, he imagines it to contain food. A person performing meaningless rituals believes he is attaining the nearness of Allah, but he is actually in a state of delusion. His senses have been numbed. He thinks that he has reached a high spiritual status, but the condition of his heart remains unclean.

Pleasure from Zikr

A sincere Ahmadi once said to me that great pleasure is derived from such practices. I told him the pleasure is similar to that derived from opium and cocaine. The conclusive proof is that such *Zikr* does not produce spiritual purity. He agreed and told me that he knew someone who had mastered all the rituals, but begged for food in the streets. The

Difference Between Zikr and Mere Influence of Thoughts

Ahmadi added that he used to wonder: if this man has reached the high status which he claims, why does he need to beg?

The Promised Messiah^{as} has narrated a story about a *Pir* (saint) who claimed that he had achieved a high spiritual status. Once while visiting a follower during a famine, the Pir demanded, "Bring my homage." The follower, who could find nothing to offer, begged to be excused, but the *Pir* kept on insisting. In the end, the follower was forced to sell some of his household effects to satisfy the *Pir's* demands.

In short, many weaknesses and impurities of heart are found in people who make pompous claims about the misguided forms of *Zikr*.

Difference Between Zikr and Mere Influence of Thoughts

God Almighty has vested human voice and thought with a special power. If a person keeps thinking that something has happened, his mind will be inclined to believe accordingly. Similarly, if someone starts imagining that his heart is emitting the sound of Allah, he begins to perceive that sound. The question arises: if the heart really produces that sound, why is it not purified?

There is an important difference between those who truly love God and those who play tricks. The difference is simple, but failure to recognize it makes a man careless about his reformation. He may believe that he has reached Allah, whereas actually he has not. Like a man who has arrived at a wrong destination but believes that he has arrived at his goal, he will sit there and suffer the loss. Those who indulge in misguided practices imagine that they have reached their true objective but actually they are miles away from it. Like an addict of opium, they are in a state of frenzied intoxication and senselessness.

The Promised Messiah^{as} urged his followers to stay away from the wrong forms of *Zikr*. He criticized those who practiced them, "How can these practices be called remembrance of Allah in a true sense when even the Hindus and Christians can practice them?"

Reciting Zikr Aloud

What about reciting *Zikr* aloud or listening to songs and music? As I mentioned earlier, the human nervous system has been granted the power to influence as well as to be influenced. The ears provide one of the paths to the nervous system. They respond to pleasing sounds. This applies not only to human beings, but also to other creatures. Play a flute to a snake, and it starts dancing. Can you say that it is under spiritual influence? Not at all! Similarly, if someone starts dancing to the tune of a song, it cannot be said that he has accepted a spiritual influence; only that his feelings have been influenced. Anyone who believes that singing has a spiritual effect is mistaken. Just as snake dances to the tune of a flute, the *Sufis* of today respond to songs and music. Moreover, it is an innovation in the faith of Islam to perform *Zikr* loudly.

Once, the Holy Prophet[saw] was traveling with his Companions. He heard them say *"AllahoAkbar, AllahoAkbar"* loudly. Hadhrat Abu Musa[ra] narrates that the Holy Prophet[saw] advised them, *"Have mercy on yourselves. Why do you not speak softly? The One Whom you are calling is not deaf or absent; He is with you and hears you well."*

The *Sufis* of today go against the directions of the Holy Prophet[saw]. When they hold meetings of *Zikr*, the whole vicinity is filled with noise. They deem it an act of goodness; whereas, in fact, they are going against the *Shari'ah* (Islamic law). Their practice—dancing, shouting, falling, and moving their heads around—do not accord with the teachings of Islam.

Poetry as Zikr?

It is said that the Holy Prophet[saw] listened to poetry, but nobody can prove that he heard poetry as remembrance of Allah. Sometimes Hadhrat Hassaan[ra] came to him saying, *"O Prophet of Allah, an opponent has composed couplets against you and I have prepared this reply."* Similarly once a person, against whom he had issued a death sentence, presented himself and after receiving permission, recited a few couplets begging forgiveness. The Holy Prophet[saw] spread his mantel over him to indicate forgiveness. Later the man said, *"I was not afraid of death, but I had recognized the truth of Islam and did not want to die as a disbeliever."* At another occasion, a Companion wrote a poem during a war in which he

Poetry as Zikr? said, "This day we will be victorious or we will accept death; but we will not retreat."

None of this shows that remembrance of Allah takes the form of rapturous songs or recital of poetry, nor does it prove that the Companion danced or got intoxicated. All these practices are innovations. The behavior, which is incited by these poems, is vulgar and un-Islamic. Islam does not condone it at all.

CHARACTERISTICS OF TRUE ZIKR ACCORDING TO ISLAMIC TEACHINGS

What Allah says about *Zikr-i-Ilahi* is the following:

... اِنَّمَا الْمُؤْمِنُوْنَ الَّذِيْنَ اِذَا ذُكِرَ اللّٰهُ وَجِلَتْ قُلُوْبُهُمْ ...

True believers are only those whose hearts tremble when the name of Allah is mentioned...(8:3)

... تَقْشَعِرُّ مِنْهُ جُلُوْدُ الَّذِيْنَ يَخْشَوْنَ رَبَّهُمْ ۚ ثُمَّ تَلِيْنُ جُلُوْدُهُمْ وَ قُلُوْبُهُمْ اِلٰى ذِكْرِ اللّٰهِ ...

...at which do creep the skins of those who fear their Lord; then their skins and their hearts soften to the remembrance of Allah...(39:24)

... اِذَا تُتْلٰى عَلَيْهِمْ اٰيٰتُ الرَّحْمٰنِ خَرُّوْا سُجَّدًا وَّبُكِيًّا *

...when the signs of the Gracious God are recited unto them, they fall down, prostrating themselves before God, weeping. (19:59)

According to these verses the attitude of those who truly remember Allah is the following:

1. Their hearts are filled with the fear of Allah because they are reminded of the status and the Glory of their God.
2. Their skins creep, that is, the hair on their bodies rise, due to their state of fear.
3. Their bodies are softened, and their hearts become tender.
4. They prostrate, that is, they start worshipping God.
5. They cry or weep.

These are the five effects mentioned in the Holy Qur'an. If dancing, jumping, falling unconscious, or shouting were appropriate conditions of Zikr, God Almighty would surely have spoken of them too. He does not mention any of them; hence, they have nothing to do with the remembrance of Allah.

True Zikr Rules Out Dancing and Shouting

Nobody can even claim that the current practices are legitimate additions to those specified by Allah, because the words used by Allah rule them out completely. The words used are: *Wajl, Iqtishar, Ta'leen,* and *Jalood.*

One of the meanings of *Wajl* is softness and erosion. That calls for a state of rest. But the *Sufis* of today move around in a state of frenzy, which contradicts this concept. Similarly, *Iqtishar* occurs when the skin creeps due to fear. That too requires a state of rest, because in a state of fear one is stunned and movement is restricted. The words *Ta'leen* and *Jalood* similarly require a state of rest.

The proper word in Arabic to indicate movement is *Turb*. It is used for chanting and jumping with joy. The word has not been used in the Holy Qur'an for remembrance of Allah. The lexicons say that the state of *Turb* is the opposite of the states of humbleness and submission, the appropriate results of remembrance of Allah.

Islam teaches rationality, wisdom, and the importance of following a straight path—not insanity and foolishness that leads to jumping, hopping, and shouting. The latter cannot be the teachings of Islam.

Unconsciousness is Not a Proper Result of Zikr

Falling unconscious is also not a proper Islamic response to extreme emotion. A Muslim experiencing a tragic death is permitted to shed tears in sorrow, but not to express loud and public wailing nor to fall unconscious. Once the Holy Prophet[saw] passed by a woman showing uncontrollable grief on the grave of her child. He advised her to be patient. She replied, "If your child had died, you would have realized how difficult it is to show patience." She spoke out of ignorance. The truth is the Holy Prophet[saw] suffered the death of several of his children. In short, wailing and falling unconscious are caused by impatience and lack of hope.

As for falling unconscious due to despair or lack of hope, Allah says:

Unconsciousness is Not a Proper Result of Zikr

... وَلَا تَايْئَسُوْا مِنْ رَّوْحِ اللّٰهِ ۖ اِنَّهٗ لَا يَايْئَسُ مِنْ رَّوْحِ اللّٰهِ اِلَّا الْقَوْمُ الْكٰفِرُوْنَ ۞

...and despair not of the mercy of Allah; for none despairs of Allah's mercy except the unbelieving people. (12:88)

Anyone who falls unconscious for lack of hope commits an act of disbelief. If he does so due to weakness of the heart, he is sick. There is no wisdom involved in either case.

The matter of unconsciousness was discussed during the time of the Companions of the Holy Prophet[saw]. Hadhrat Abdullah bin Zubair[ra] asked Hadhrat Asmaa[ra] about unconsciousness. She replied, "I seek refuge with Allah from Satan the accursed." The son of Hadhrat Abdullah bin Zubair[ra] narrated that he saw people falling unconscious upon hearing the recitation of the Holy Qur'an. Hadhrat Asma'a[ra] who was the daughter of Hadhrat Abu Bakr[ra] and a Companion of the Holy Prophet[saw], responded, "If you saw this, you witnessed a Satanic act."

Ibn Sirin, author of the well-known book on the interpretation of dreams, was the son-in-law of Hadhrat Abu Hurairah[ra] He was once told about someone who fell unconscious upon hearing a verse of the Holy Qur'an. He replied, "Put him on a high wall and then read to him the whole Qur'an, not just one verse. If he falls unconscious, I will agree that he is influenced by the recitation of the Holy Qur'an."

Even now, those who feign unconsciousness carefully avoid injury. Except by mistake, they do not fall from a roof or to a place where they might get hurt. Generally, they fall upon other people in a crowd.

In short, all innovations introduced into *Zikr* are wrong and forbidden. They deserve to be condemned because they destroy spirituality. They degrade men to the status of monkeys and bears. Islam wants to raise men beyond the status of angels and considers these practices to be vain and useless.

Four Kinds of Zikr Enjoined by Islam

Zikr, as enjoined by the Holy Qur'an, is of four types. All of these should be observed diligently; missing any of them will deprive one of a great blessing. The four types are as follows.

1. The prescribed Prayers;
2. Recitation of the Holy Qur'an;
3. Reciting the attributes of Allah, acknowledging their truthfulness, and verbalizing their details; and
4. Publicly proclaiming the attributes of Allah.

The importance of these four types of *Zikr* is well established in the Holy Qur'an. They are important, indeed vital, for attaining spiritual progress.

Now I will prove that these four types of *Zikr* are enjoined by the Holy Qur'an. God Almighty says about Prayer:

$$\text{اِنَّنِیْۤ اَنَا اللّٰهُ لَاۤ اِلٰهَ اِلَّاۤ اَنَا فَاعۡبُدۡنِیۡ وَ اَقِمِ الصَّلٰوةَ لِذِکۡرِیۡ}$$

Verily, I am Allah; there is no God besides Me, so worship Me alone, and observe Prayer for My remembrance. (20:15)

This verse shows that when Allah says, remember Me, He means observe the Prayer (*Salat*). Then Allah says:

$$\text{فَاِنۡ خِفۡتُمۡ فَرِجَالًا اَوۡ رُکۡبَانًا ۚ فَاِذَاۤ اَمِنۡتُمۡ فَاذۡکُرُوا اللّٰهَ کَمَا عَلَّمَکُمۡ مَّا لَمۡ تَکُوۡنُوۡا تَعۡلَمُوۡنَ}$$

If you are in a state of fear, then say your Prayers on foot or riding; but when you are safe, remember Allah as He has taught you that which you did not know. (2:240)

In this verse the observance of *Salat* has been called remembrance of Allah.

There are many other verses, but these two will suffice for now. The second *Zikr* is recitation of the Holy Qur'an. Allah says:

Four Kinds of Zikr Enjoined by Islam

$$\text{اِنَّا نَحْنُ نَزَّلْنَا الذِّكْرَ وَاِنَّا لَهُ لَحٰفِظُوْنَ}$$

Verily, We Ourself have sent down this Exhortation, and We will, most surely, safeguard it. (15:10)

In this verse the revelation of the Holy Qur'an has been called the descent of the Exhortation—*Zikr* in the Arabic text. Hence, when Allah says remember Allah; He also means recite the Holy Qur'an. The Allah says:

$$\text{وَهٰذَا ذِكْرٌ مُّبٰرَكٌ اَنْزَلْنٰهُ اَفَاَنْتُمْ لَهٗ مُنْكِرُوْنَ}$$

And this is the blessed reminder that We have sent down; will you then reject it? (21:51)

This verse represents the Holy Qur'an as a reminder; the Arabic word used here too is *"Zikr"*.

The third form of *Zikr* consists of reciting the attributes of Allah, and acknowledging their truthfulness. Some people believe that it is sufficient to recite the attributes of Allah during *Salat*. This is wrong. Remembrance of Allah—in addition to *Salat*—is clearly enjoined by the Holy Qur'an. Allah says:

$$\text{فَاِذَا قَضَيْتُمُ الصَّلٰوةَ فَاذْكُرُوا اللّٰهَ قِيَامًا وَّ قُعُوْدًا وَّعَلٰى جُنُوْبِكُمْ ...}$$

(And) when you have finished the Prayer, remember Allah while standing, and sitting, and lying, on your sides... (4:104)

Clearly, the *Zikr* mentioned here is in addition to *Salat*. Then Allah says:

$$\text{رِجَالٌ لَّا تُلْهِيْهِمْ تِجَارَةٌ وَّلَا بَيْعٌ عَنْ ذِكْرِ اللّٰهِ وَاِقَامِ الصَّلٰوةِ وَاِيْتَاءِ الزَّكٰوةِ يَخَافُوْنَ يَوْمًا تَتَقَلَّبُ فِيْهِ الْقُلُوْبُ وَالْاَبْصَارُ}$$

Four Kinds of Zikr Enjoined by Islam

By men, whom neither merchandises nor traffic diverts from the remembrance of Allah and the observance of Prayer, and the giving of *Zakat*. They fear a day in which hearts and eyes will be agitated. (24:38)

Here again remembrance of Allah is distinct from the *Salat*.

The fourth kind of *Zikr* is the public proclamation of the attributes of Allah. He says:

$$\text{يَاۤ اَيُّهَا الْمُدَّثِّرُ * قُمْ فَاَنْذِرْ * وَرَبَّكَ فَكَبِّرْ * وَثِيَابَكَ فَطَهِّرْ * وَالرُّجْزَ فَاهْجُرْ * وَلَا تَمْنُنْ تَسْتَكْثِرُ * وَلِرَبِّكَ فَاصْبِرْ *}$$

O Thou that has wrapped thyself with the mantle! Arise and warn. And thy Lord do thou magnify. And thy heart do thou purify. And uncleanliness do thou shun. And bestow not favors seeking to get more in return. And for the sake of thy Lord do thou endure patiently. (74:2–8)

Methods of Performing Zikr

What are the proper methods of performing these forms of *Zikr*? The different types of *Zikr* can be divided into two groups: obligatory, and voluntary. By the grace of God, our Community is very mindful of the obligatory form of *Zikr*; I will not discuss it much. Later in the discussion I will say something about *Nawafil*, the voluntary form, which requires extensive discussion. Let me start with how the Holy Qur'an should be recited.

Recitation of the Holy Qur'an

1. The Holy Qur'an should be recited regularly and according to a set plan. Fix a portion for daily reading rather than picking up the Holy Qur'an once in a while and reading at random. Irregular reading does not yield any benefit. Whether you decide upon half a part for your daily reading, or a full part, or a few of them, the determined quota of reading must be recited daily without any laxity. The Holy Prophet[saw] says, "Allah loves worship which is performed regularly and is never missed."

Irregularity indicates lack of enthusiasm, and the heart cannot be purified without enthusiasm and true love. My personal experience confirms this point. Whenever I am very busy in writing a book or due to another engagement and cannot recite the Holy Qur'an, my heart feels anguish and other modes of worship are also adversely affected.

In short the Holy Qur'an should be recited daily...

Expressing the Greatness and Glory of Allah and Thanking Him

2. Try to understand what you are reading. The Holy Qur'an should not be recited hurriedly. Slow recitation will enable you to understand, and will also show proper respect for the Holy Qur'an.

An Ahmadi once asked what to do if one does not understand the meanings of the Holy Qur'an. Such people should learn the meanings of a portion of the Holy Qur'an and should include that portion in every recitation. You may ask: What is the benefit of reciting the parts which we do not understand? Remember that when something is done with sincerity and good intention, Allah definitely rewards it. If you recite for the sake of God without knowing the meanings, He will certainly bless you according to your sincerity. Moreover, the words have an influence. The Holy Prophet[saw] has commanded that *Adhan* (call for formal Islamic Prayer) be recited in the ears of the newborn child. The child is unable to understand or recognize anything at that time, but it is influenced by the words of the *Adhan*.

3. As far as possible, perform ablution before recitation. I consider it permissible to recite the Holy Qur'an without ablution, but some scholars consider it undesirable. It is certainly more appropriate to perform ablution to obtain greater benefit and to earn higher reward.

Expressing the Greatness and Glory of Allah and Thanking Him

Another form of *Zikr* consists of *Tasbeeh* (proclaiming the Glory of Allah), *Tahmeed* (expressing thankfulness to Allah) and *Takbeer* (proclaiming the Greatness of Allah). Such *Zikr* can be performed alone or in company.

Sometimes such *Zikr* is obligatory, like saying the *Takbeer*, that is, *AllahoAkbar* (Allah is the Greatest) while slaughtering an animal. If the *Takbeer* is not proclaimed, the slaughter will not accord with the Islamic instructions. But *Tasbeeh* and *Tahmeed* is also repeated in low voice as remembrance of Allah.

The Holy Prophet[saw] has prescribed some form of *Zikr* for every occasion:

- When beginning a meal, he has taught us to say:

بِسْمِ اللّٰهِ الرَّحْمٰنِ الرَّحِيْمِ

Bismillah ir Rahman ir Raheem
In the name of Allah, Most Gracious Ever-Merciful. (1:1)

Expressing the Greatness and Glory of Allah and Thanking Him

Anyone who does not say *"Bismillah…"* will also fills his stomach. But the true objective of eating will only be satisfied with *"Bismillah…"* There will be spiritual benefits in the meal.

- At the completion of every activity, the Holy Prophet[saw] has taught us to say:

* اَلْحَمْدُ لِلّٰهِ رَبِّ الْعَالَمِيْنَ ۙ

Alhamdolillah Rabbil-Aalameen
All Praise belongs to Allah, Lord of all the worlds. (1:2)

Alhamdolillah is also recited when wearing new clothes or when one is bestowed any other blessing.

- On every occasion of sorrow we are taught to pray:

*… اِنَّا لِلّٰهِ وَ اِنَّآ اِلَيْهِ رٰجِعُوْنَ

…Inna Lillahi wa inna Ilaihi raji'un
To Allah we belong and to Him shall we return… (2:157)

- When faced with a task beyond his ability, a Muslim is taught to pray:

لَاحَوْلَ وَلَا قُوَّةَ اِلَّا بِاللّٰه

La haula wa la quwwata Illa billah
There is no scheme nor any power except with the help of Allah.

These forms of *Zikr* encompass all aspects of life. Either joy or sorrow can be experienced during the day. When faced with joy, a Muslim says: *Alhamdolillah Rabbil-Aalameen* (All Praise belongs to Allah, Lord of all the worlds). If in sorrow, he says: *Inna Lillahi wa inna Ilaihi raji'un* (to Allah we

Proclaiming Unity of Allah as Zikr belong and to Him shall we return). The Holy Prophet[saw] has prescribed *Zikr* for every occasion, in accordance with the commandment of Almighty Allah, Who says:

$$\ldots \text{فَاذْكُرُوا اللّٰهَ قِيَامًا وَّ قُعُودًا وَّعَلٰى جُنُوبِكُمْ} \ldots$$

...remember Allah while standing, sitting, or lying on your sides... (4:104)

If you follow these directions, you will always be engaged in remembrance of Allah. If you hear good news while working in your office, say *Alhamdolillah*. If you hear such news while walking, say *Alhamdolillah*. Repeat *Tahmeed* if the happy news comes while lying down. Thus, remembrance of Allah will continue in every situation.

Proclaiming Unity of Allah as Zikr

The Holy Prophet[saw] has also said (as narrated by Jabir in *Book of Tirmidhi*), that the best and the foremost way of remembering Allah is to proclaim:

$$\text{لَآ اِلٰهَ اِلَّا اللّٰهُ}$$

La Ilaha Illallah
There is none worthy of worship except Allah.

Other Recitations

There are other forms of *Zikr*, which are very meritorious. An important recitation is:[1]

$$\text{سُبْحَانَ اللّٰهِ وَ بِحَمْدِهٖ سُبْحَانَ اللّٰهِ الْعَظِيْمِ}$$

Subhan Allahi wa bi Hamdihi, Subhan Allahil-Azeem
Holy is Allah, with His Praise;
Holy is Allah, the Greatess

Concerning this recitation the Holy Prophet[saw] says, "There are two sentences which are very easy to say, but they will weigh heavily on the

---

1. Narrated by *Bukhari* and *Muslim*.

scale of good deeds on the Day of Judgement. They are very dear to the Gracious Lord." They constitute *Zikr* of very high order.

Once the Promised Messiah[as] was unwell but woke up for *Tahajjud*. Because of weakness he could not stand up for *Tahajjud*. He received a revelation that he could nonetheless achieve great merit by reciting the above *Zikr* in that condition. It is narrated in the sayings of the Holy Prophet[saw] that he used to recite it very often.

The Holy Prophet[saw] has told us about the superiority of these forms of *Zikr*. There is another recitation, which is very meritorious; even though no Hadith has been preserved about it, reason guides us towards its merit. This *Zikr* consists of reciting the verses of the Holy Qur'an by way of remembrance of Allah. It is doubly blessed because it brings a reward for reciting the Holy Qur'an as well as of performing *Zikr*.

Other Recitations

Precautions and Proper Times for this Form of Zikr

Having stated the nature and the forms of *Zikr*, I will now deal with the necessary precautions and proper times for performing *Zikr*.

Necessary Precautions for Zikr

1. The Holy Prophet[saw] has instructed us not to prolong *Zikr* to the point of fatigue.

2. Do not engage in *Zikr* when the mind is unsettled. Trying to perform *Zikr* in the midst of some important assignment is not advisable. The effort would be half-hearted and disrespectful to the words of God; it will count as a sin.

To reiterate: perform *Zikr* briefly and with full attention.

Once when the Holy Prophet[saw] came home, Hadhrat A'isha[ra] was talking to a lady. Hadhrat A'isha[ra] told the Holy Prophet[saw] that the lady spent long hours in worship. He answered, "There is no merit in carrying worship to such extremes. Allah is pleased with worship that is constant. Allah does not get tired, but a person does get tired with excess of worship. The worship is then performed without zeal and good spirits, and earns no merit. If someone exceeds the limit, he brings distress upon himself."

Hadhrat Abdullah bin Umar bin Aus[ra] was a healthy man. He prayed all night, fasted during the day, and recited the whole of Holy Qur'an in one day. When the Holy Prophet[saw] heard about it, he said, "This is not right. Pray for one sixth, one third, or at the most, half of the night. Fast on alternate days. Do not complete the recitation of the Holy Qur'an in less than three days." Abdullah bin Umar bin Aus[ra] begged for more, but

Necessary Precautions for Zikr

was not permitted. He pledged to carry out the maximum permitted. He kept his pledge for a long time, but in his old age, he regretted that he had not availed himself of the further concessions.

Anything carried to extremes causes problems. Too much of good food will upset the stomach; similarly excess *Zikr* causes fatigue and aversion. Increase the demand upon your self gradually and limit them to your capabilities.

3. If you cannot concentrate in the beginning, remain steadfast and complete your quota despite Satanic insinuations. With resolute determination, you can overcome your weaknesses.

Tacon, a famous lawyer, was once pleading a case. The opposing lawyer, fearing that Tacon would win the case, employed a clever stratagem. While speaking with the magistrate, he said, "Tacon claims that he can get a favorable judgement from any magistrate irrespective of the merits of the case." The magistrate made up his mind not to listen to Tacon. When the proceedings started, the magistrate denied every submission that Tacon made. Finally, he gave a verdict in favor of the other party. In conclusion, no one can influence a person who has resolved not to be influenced. In the initial stages of acquiring the habit of *Zikr*, cultivate the attitude of concentration to avert all extraneous influences.

4. Do not perform *Zikr* in a condition of physical discomfort. If something hurts you, get rid of it before starting *Zikr*.

5. Accept cheerfully whatever you are granted. Even if you do not achieve perfect concentration in the beginning, a time will come when the habit of *Zikr* will be well established.

6. Perform *Zikr* with humbleness and fear of Allah. If you do not experience true humility, simulate a corresponding facial expression; the desired state of mind will follow. It often happens that someone adopts a manner artificially, but gradually acquires it as second nature. If you simulate humbleness and weeping, you will soon develop humbleness of spirit.

It is narrated a professor was very kind-hearted, but later became very cruel. This was how it happened. Due to his mild nature, one day he suffered a loss, and resolved thenceforth to be firm. So he adopted a firm demeanor, even though deep down, he was still kind-hearted. Gradually harshness took root in his character. The professor moved towards evil by using the principle of simulation, but it can be used to move towards virtue as well. On the first day true humbleness may appear only for a fleeting moment; the second day, it will stay longer. In due course, the results of sustained effort will be quite visible.

Necessary Precautions for Zikr

There are some other general points, which need to be re-iterated.

Except on occasions permissible according to Hadith, do not perform *Zikr* loudly. This can create pretence, and can distract others from remembering Allah or performing *Salat*.

Remember that new practices are difficult to adopt. Getting used to them takes time. Many people complain that they cannot put their hearts into *Zikr*. Well, do you think that anyone can master a new skill in a day? Not at all! It takes time and patience. Therefore, if you find it difficult in the beginning, do not be discouraged. You will get used to it gradually. The only condition is to remain steadfast.

Some say that they relish *Zikr*. They should not seek pleasure in *Zikr*, but should perform it as worship, which is the real objective. Worship is accepted only when it is performed with that intention.

Some complain that they feel uninterested in *Zikr* for days and then begin to feel interested. To them my advice is: Do not be discouraged, because this is a common experience. Once a Companion came to the Holy Prophet[saw] and said, "O my Master, I am a hypocrite." He responded, "No you are a Muslim." He submitted, "When I come to your presence, I can witness Heaven and Hell, but when I go back, I lose that spirit." He said, "If you remain in the same condition all the time, you will soon die."

Remaining in the same condition stifles the capacity to advance. At times, God Almighty lowers a person from his true status to make him advance in an effort to regain his position; similarly, He sometimes lets him enjoy the higher status to motivate him to acquire it on a permanent basis.

Lack of interest may, however, be either beneficial or harmful. The difference between the two can be recognized. Assume that there are degrees of interest in performing *Zikr;* zero indicating total absence of interest and stages one through five indicating progressively higher stages. If you are at stage two and lack of interest does not lower you below stage one, then it is of the beneficial kind. From stage three, if it brings you not

Proper Times for Zikr

lower than stage two, then it is the beneficial kind; however if it lowers you to stage one or zero then you should be concerned and make an extra effort to maintain your position.

Proper Times for Zikr

The above proves conclusively that *Zikr* is extremely essential. As I mentioned earlier, God Almighty says:

$$\text{فَاِذَا قَضَيْتُمُ الصَّلٰوةَ فَاذْكُرُوا اللّٰهَ قِيَامًا وَّ قُعُوْدًا وَّعَلٰى جُنُوْبِكُمْ} \ldots$$

And when you have fished the Prayer, remember Allah while standing and sitting, and lying on your sides… (4:104)

An important question arises: What are the right times for *Zikr*? In a sense, Allah should be remembered all the times. Hadhrat A'isha[ra] says that, "The Holy Prophet[saw] used to remember Allah all the time." But certain times have been specified in the Holy Qur'an. For example:

$$\text{وَاذْكُرِ اسْمَ رَبِّكَ بُكْرَةً وَّاَصِيْلًا}$$

And remember Allah at the time of *Bukra* and *Aseel*. (76:26)

The times specified in this verse are very important. *Bukra*, in Arabic means the time from the first flush of dawn to sunrise. In other words, Allah should be remembered from Morning Prayer till sunrise. *Aseel*, the other time specified for *Zikr*, is from late Afternoon Prayer (*Asr*) up to sunset.

God Almighty also says:

$$\text{فَاصْبِرْ عَلٰى مَا يَقُوْلُوْنَ وَ سَبِّحْ بِحَمْدِ رَبِّكَ قَبْلَ طُلُوْعِ الشَّمْسِ وَقَبْلَ غُرُوْبِهَا وَ مِنْ اٰنَآئِ الَّيْلِ فَسَبِّحْ وَاَطْرَافَ النَّهَارِ لَعَلَّكَ تَرْضٰى}$$

Bear patiently then what they say, and glorify thy Lord with His praise before the rising of the sun and before its setting; and glorify Him in the hours of the night and at the sides of the day, that thou mayest find true happiness. (20:131)

This verse identifies three additional times for remembrance of Allah: the time after sunrise, and the first and the last part of the night.

The sixth time for the remembrance of Allah is immediately after each prescribed Prayer. The Holy Prophet[saw] was very diligent about *Zikr* at this time. To perform *Zikr* at this time is his *Sunnah* (tradition). Hadhrat Ibn Abbas[ra] says that the Companions who were late for Prayers could tell from the following sound of *Zikr* that the Prayer service had been concluded.

اَنْتَ السَّلَامُ وَمِنْكَ السَّلَامُ يَا ذَاالْجَلَالِ وَالْاِكْرَامِ

Thou art Peace, O Allah, and all peace emanates from Thee, O Possessor of Majesty and Lofty Station.

The other form of *Zikr* after Prayers consisted of reciting:

سُبْحَانَ اللهِ

Subhan-Allah (All Glory belongs to Allah)

اَلْحَمْدُ لِلّٰهِ

Alhamdolillah (All Praise belongs to Allah)

اَللّٰهُ اَكْبَرُ

AllahoAkbar (Allah is the Greatest)

There are several traditions about this *Zikr*. The best way to perform is to recite the first phrase thirty-three times, then the second phrase thirty-three times, and finally the third phrase thirty-four times.

The time after Prayer has great merit for *Zikr* and should be fully utilized. Some people may be under the impression that I do not perform this *Zikr* or that Hadhrat Khalifatul-Masih I[ra] or the Promised Messiah[as] did not perform it. This is wrong. The Promised Messiah[as] did it and so did Hadhrat Khalifatul-Masih I[ra]. However, they did not do it loudly, nor do I. You, too, should make it a habit.

The Prayers

I will now turn to the most important form of *Zikr*: the prescribed Prayers. In Prayers a Muslim perform *Zikr*, in all the postures—standing (*Qiyam*), bowing down (*Ruku'*), prostration (*Sajdah*), and sitting (*Qa'adah*). He recites the Holy Qur'an and perform other types of *Zikr*. A Prayer is a combination of all forms of *Zikr*.

The Philosophy of Prescribing Sunnah and Nawafil

The prescribed Prayers have three parts (1) *Fard*, the obligatory part, (2) *Sunnah*, the part offered regularly by the Holy Prophet[saw] and enjoined by him, and (3) *Nawafil*, the voluntary part. Most of the people regularly perform only *Fard* and *Sunnah*.

The *Sunnah* has been instituted to offset shortcomings in the obligatory parts. Allah does not accept defective Prayers; He only accepts the flawless. But He accepts *Sunnah* in lieu of defects in the *Fard*. If one of the *Raka'at* (component part) in the *Fard* Prayer lacks concentration, or is spoiled by temptations, it will not be accepted. But the loss will be offset with *Sunnah*. The Holy Prophet[saw] had a very keen awareness of human nature and its frailties. He has done a great favor to his followers by adding *Sunnah* in the Prayers.

Then there are *Nawafil*. These are means of attaining nearness to God. They raise a man above *Najat* (deliverance from sin). Anyone desiring nearness of Allah should give special attention to *Nawafil*. Some *Nawafil* are performed during the day; others during the night. Those performed at night—*Tahajjud*—carry special blessings. God Almighty says:

$$\text{اِنَّ نَاشِئَةَ الَّيْلِ هِىَ اَشَدُّ وَطْاً وَّاَقْوَمُ قِيْلًا}$$

How to Get Up at Night for Tahajjud

Verily getting up at night is the most potent means of subduing the self and most effective in respect of words of Prayer. (73:7)

The self can be reformed and great spiritual heights scaled with *Tahajjud*. Anyone who performs it will discover its importance. The Companions of the Holy Prophet[saw] were very regular in saying *Tahajjud*. Even though it is voluntary, the Holy Prophet[saw] used to walk around to see who observed it. Once, good qualities of Hadhrat Abdullah bin Umar[ra] were being mentioned. The Holy Prophet[saw] said, "Yes, he is very good, but he should also offer *Tahajjud*." The Holy Prophet[saw] thus reminded him of his slackness in observing the *Tahajjud* Prayers.

The Holy Prophet[saw] has said, "May Allah have mercy on the husband and the wife who awake each other up for Prayer at night. If the husband wakes, let him offer *Tahajjud* and awaken his wife. If she does not get up, let him sprinkle some water at her face. Similarly, if the wife awakes, let her do the same, that is, offer *Tahajjud* and awaken her husband by sprinkling some water at his face." The Holy Prophet[saw] has directed the wife to respect her husband. Yet he has permitted her to sprinkle some water, if necessary, to awaken him for *Tahajjud*. Obviously, he attaches great importance to *Tahajjud*.

The Holy Qur'an tells us that getting up for Prayer at night straightens the self. According to the Holy Prophet[saw] you must perform *Tahajjud*, even if it is of two *Raka'at*. He also says that God Almighty accepts the prayers in abundance during the late part of night. *Tahajjud*, therefore, is very important and beneficial.

How to Get Up at Night for Tahajjud

One way—not very useful in my opinion—is to use the alarm clock. It creates dependency, and fails to produce the resolute will. If you go to sleep having resolved to get up for *Tahajjud,* you will be in a state of worship all night. Being determined, you will get up. Those depending on the alarm clock, but lacking determination, will often shut the alarm clock to go back to sleep. When they get up, they generally feel sleepy in Prayers. Their dependency prevents them from full awakening and alertness. However, under certain circumstances the alarm clock may be used by beginners or others.

There are thirteen methods, which can help in getting up at night. Anyone who sincerely tries them will, God willing, benefit from them. There may be difficulties in the beginning, but in the end these methods will prove useful. I have derived these methods from the Holy Qur'an and *Hadiths*. It is Allah's Grace that these points, which remained hidden from others, have been manifested to me. To save time, I will only give my conclusions without quoting the references.

How to Get Up at Night for Tahajjud

1. It is a law of nature that everything reverts to its original state if similar circumstances reappear. Often, in old age a person suffers from his childhood diseases. The same happens to birds and trees. This law can be helpful in cultivating the habit of getting up during the night. Perform *Zikr* for a while after *Isha* Prayers. The more *Zikr* you perform, the earlier you will get up for *Zikr* before the morning.

2. Do not talk to anybody after *Isha* Prayers. Although sometimes the Holy Prophet[saw] continued his conversation after *Isha*, as a general rule he had forbidden it. There are two reasons: (a) if you start talking, you will sleep late and will not be able to get up early in the morning; and (b) if the conversation concerns things other than faith, your attention will be diverted. You should go to sleep while thinking of your faith; you will get up with the same thoughts. It is not forbidden to carry out office work or other important assignments after *Isha*. But in that case it is better to spend some time in *Zikr* before going to sleep.

3. Perform *Wudu* (ablution) before going to bed, even if you are already in a state of ablution. It affects the heart and creates a special kind of freshness. If you go to sleep in that state of freshness, you will get up in the same condition. This is a common observation. Someone smiling at bedtime is generally smiling when he gets up; one, who is crying, will wake up crying. With ablution you will be fresh at the time of sleep and fresh when you wake up. It will also help you in getting up.

4. Recite some *Zikr* before falling asleep; this will cause you to wake up again for *Zikr* during the night. The Holy Prophet[saw] used to perform *Zikr* in the following manner before going to sleep: He recited *Ayatul-Kursi* (verse 2:256) and the last three chapters of the

How to Get Up at Night for Tahajjud

Holy Qur'an; he then gently blew upon his hands and lightly passed them over his body three times. Then he turned towards his right and said:

اَللّٰهُمَّ اَسْلَمْتُ نَفْسِیْ اِلَیْکَ وَوَجَّهْتُ وَجْهِیْ اِلَیْکَ وَ فَوَّضْتُ اَمْرِیْ اِلَیْکَ رَغْبَةً وَّرَهْبَةً اِلَیْکَ لَا مَلْجَاً وَلَامَنْجَاً مِنْکَ اِلَّا اِلَیْکَ اَللّٰهُمَّ اٰمَنْتُ بِکِتَابِکَ الَّذِیْ اَنْزَلْتَ وَنَبِیِّکَ الَّذِیْ اَرْسَلْتَ

Allahumma inni aslamto nafsi ilaik. Wa wajjahtu waj hi ilaik. Wa fawwadtu amri ilaik raghbatan wa rahbatan ilaik. La malja'a wa la manja'a minka illa ilaik. Allahumma aamanto bikitabikalladhi anzalta wa nabiyyikalladhi arsalta.

O Allah, I put myself in Thy protection, and turn my face towards Thee and assign all my affairs to Thee, with complete inclination and fear of Thee. There is no refuge or protection from Thee except towards Thyself. I believe in Thy Book, which Thou hast revealed, and Thy Prophet that Thou hast sent.

All believers should perform this *Zikr* and then continue with another form of *Zikr* until sleep takes over. An important recitation for this time is:

سُبْحَانَ اللّٰهِ وَ بِحَمْدِهٖ سُبْحَانَ اللّٰهِ الْعَظِیْم

Subhan Allahi wa bi Hamdihi, Subhan Allahil-Azeem
Holy is Allah, with His Praise;
Holy is Allah, the Greatess

The condition in which a person goes to sleep stays with him all night. If someone sleeps while performing *Tasbeeh* (Glorification of God) and *Tahmeed* (Praise of God) he will remain in that spiritual state all night. It is a common observation that ladies or children, who are disturbed or are in pain at bedtime cry when they turn over onto their sides during sleep.

Similarly, if someone goes to sleep reciting *Tasbeeh* he will recite *Tasbeeh* when he will turn his side. God Almighty says:

How to Get Up at Night for Tahajjud

$$\text{تَتَجَافٰى جُنُوْبُهُمْ عَنِ الْمَضَاجِعِ يَدْعُوْنَ رَبَّهُمْ خَوْفًاوَّطَمَعًا وَّمِمَّا رَزَقْنٰهُمْ يُنْفِقُوْنَ}$$

Their sides keep away from their beds; and they call on their Lord in fear and hope, and spend out of what We have bestowed on them. (32:17)

To a casual observer, it may not appear that Muslims keep away from their beds. The Holy Prophet[saw] went to sleep and so do all the Muslims. But in truth their sleep is not sleep; it is a form of *Tasbeeh*. They appear to be sleeping, but in reality they are not. Their sides keep away from their beds; they are busy in the remembrance of their Lord.

5. Resolve firmly at bedtime to get up for *Tahajjud*. God Almighty has given man the power to make his mind obey his will. Philosophers have accepted this principle. Decide firmly that you will get up for *Tahajjud*. While your body sleeps, your mind will be alert. It will wake you up exactly at the desired time.

6. The sixth method is only for those who are really strong in faith. Instead of performing *Vitr* (three *Raka'at* prescribed as essential) after *Isha*, leave *Vitr* for *Tahajjud* time. In general, people are regular in performing the obligatory worship, but show slackness in the voluntary. *Vitr* are *Wajib*—an essential act of worship, not obligatory but more important than the voluntary. When a *Wajib* is combined with the *Nawafil* it would strengthen the resolve to observe both. The soul will not rest until the *Wajib* has been observed. So the *Nawafil* will also be observed. One who has already performed *Vitr* may not get up for *Tahajjud* even if he is awake. His soul will feel at ease. But if the *Vitr* are still due, the soul will be restless and will awaken him. Only the strong in faith should practice this method; the weak ones may deprive themselves even of the *Vitr* by doing so.

7. The seventh method is also for those who have excelled in spirituality. They should start offering *Nawafil* after *Isha* Prayer and continue until they begin to doze off in Prayers and are overpowered

How to Get Up at Night for Tahajjud

by sleep. Even though the total amount of their sleep will be reduced, they will find themselves awake at the time of *Tahajjud*. This method is an exercise for the spirit.

8. The eighth method has been practiced by many *Sufis*. I have not felt the need for it myself; but it is beneficial. If you get into the habit of oversleeping, then change the soft bed to a hard one.

9. Take dinner several hours before going to bed. Eat before *Maghrib* Prayer or immediately after it. Sometimes the spirit is active, but the body is not. The body acts like a yoke: if the yoke is too heavy, it strangles the spirit. The stomach should not be full at bedtime. It has an adverse affect upon the heart and makes a man lazy.

10. Do not go to bed unclean. Angels associate with those who are clean; they do not approach the unclean. Once, the Holy Prophet[saw] was offered something with a strong odor. He did not eat it, but permitted his Companions to do so. He explained to them that the angels, who visit him frequently, did not like such odors.

Angels abhor filth. Once Hadhrat Khalifatul-Masih I[ra] went to bed without washing his hands after dinner. He saw a dream. His elder brother wanted to present him the Holy Qur'an, but when he was about to touch it, his brother withdrew it and said, "Do not touch the Holy Qur'an; your hands are not clean."

Physical cleanliness affects purity of the heart. Those who are clean will have the help of angels to get up; the unclean will not be approached by them. So keep your bodies clean.

11. The bed should be clean. Many people ignore this matter. Remember that spirituality is directly influenced by cleanliness of the bed. Take special care in this respect.

12. Husband and wife should avoid going to sleep in the same bed. Amongst ordinary Muslims, this habit can harm spirituality, but it does not affect the spiritually advanced. The Holy Prophet[saw] slept in the same bed with his wives. He possessed a lofty spiritual status and his spirituality could not be compromised. Ordinary Muslims should be careful. A carnal passion adversely affects spirituality.

That is why Islam teaches:

$$...\text{كُلُوْا وَاشْرَبُوْا وَلَا تُسْرِفُوْا}...*$$

...eat and drink but exceed not the bounds... (7:32)

Why does Islam prohibit us from exceeding the limits? Because it harms spirituality. People with self-control will not suffer by sleeping together, but ordinary Muslims may find that it keeps their minds inclined towards passion. That hurts spirituality and prevents them from getting up.

13. The last method is really superior. It helps in getting up for *Tahajjud* and saves one from many sins and weaknesses. Before retiring for sleep, ponder if you have any malice or harbor any rancor or prejudices against anybody. If so, remove it. The purification achieved by this exercise will enable you to get up for *Tahajjud*.

The heart should be totally clean at bedtime. Anybody who considers such thought to be of some worth, should remind himself that he may be free to indulge in them during the day; but he has no need for them at night. After all, he is not going to fight anybody during the night.

Once rooted out, such thoughts will generally not recur. Even if they do, their damage will not be very serious. The result of a thing depends on how long it has been influenced by something else. If you wipe something with a sponge, it will be moist. But if you soak the sponge for a long time, it will be drenched. Thoughts that linger and are repeated in your mind all night would overpower your heart.

Such thoughts cannot do much harm during the day because the mind is absorbed in other activities. But during the night the mind is free to be influenced. Eliminate all bad thoughts against others which occur at bedtime, lest they become rooted. To get rid of them will then not be difficult. Moreover, should you breathe your last during the night; you will miss the opportunity of asking forgiveness for this sin.

Once you eliminate the rancor, you will be free from it permanently.. When you purify yourself at night, you will definitely be blessed with the opportunity of getting up for *Tahajjud*.

Concentrating in Prayers

I will now speak about maintaining concentration in Prayers—a subject about which I have been asked often. You may already be practicing some of the methods I will describe. If you have done full justice to them, you must have tasted their beneficent result.

As a part of the Prayer service, the *Shari'ah* (Islamic Law) has prescribed some rules for maintaining concentration. Due to their own ignorance, many people derive no benefit from these rules. I will add some techniques, which are generally not known but can be helpful.

Let me start with a general principle. When someone really believes in a technique that he is using, he receives greater benefit from it. Sando was a master body builder in Europe. He said that, "Exercise is essential for health, but at the same time you must believe that your arms and muscles are getting stronger and firmer." The arms get stronger with exercise, but when you add the belief that the body is benefiting, it is naturally influenced. Without such a belief, much of the potential impact is lost and the benefit is reduced.

Rules within Islamic Law, which Helps in Concentration

Some rules embodied in Islamic *Shari'ah* for maintaining concentration are as follows:

1. Performance of Wu*du* (ablution) is essential before starting every Prayer. God Almighty has created means of communicating thoughts and feelings. One of them is the nervous system; it acts as a channel to carry one man's feelings to the other. The Holy Prophet[saw] recited *Ayatul-Kursi* and he then blew upon his hands and lightly passed them over his body. Do you think that this was a frivolous act? No! The truth is that thoughts are channeled from one person to the other through the nervous system, the voice, and the breath. The Holy Prophet[saw] brought all channels under control by reciting *Ayatul-Kursi* with his tongue, then by blowing upon his hands, and then by lightly passing his hands over his body.

In brief, the voice, the nervous system, the sight, and the breath are all means for the expression of thoughts. That is why the righteous Muslims, including the Holy Prophet^{saw} recited specific words to achieve full spiritual benefit while blowing upon or touching the bodies.

Concentrating in Prayers

Since the nervous system is a channel for the expression of thoughts, the Holy Prophet^{saw} has instructed us to perform ablution in order to purify our thoughts. The main outlets for the expression of thoughts are the mouths, the arms and the feet which are required to be cleaned. Experiments show that when the mouth, arms and legs are washed with water, the string of evil thoughts is broken.

Ablution breaks the string of extraneous thoughts and creates tranquility and comfort. This, in turn, helps in concentrating. When you make ablution, resolve firmly that with it you are going to banish all stray thoughts. With this attitude you will experience added comfort and your thoughts will not be distracted.

2. Another means of achieving concentration in Prayers is to offer congregational Prayers at the mosque.

Human thoughts work through a process of association. When Tom meets Dick he asks him about his son Harry. Even though Harry is not present, meeting Dick reminds him of Harry. That is how the human brain works: when you see something, you also remember other things associated with it. If someone offers Prayers at a place called the house of God, where Prayers are offered day and night, he will surely think that he is standing before God for Whose worship the place has been constructed. He will thus feel that he must obey his Lord with a true heart.

The Holy Prophet^{saw} has instructed that Muslims should reserve a place for Prayer in their homes. Praying there will remind them that place is also reserved for worship.

There may be some among you who have never experienced such thoughts in the mosques. But now that the point has been made clear to you, you will be able to go to mosques with these feelings. This will help you to control wayward thoughts, concentrate on your act of worship, and find true peace.

3. The instruction to face towards *Ka'aba* (the first house of God built in Mecca) also helps in achieving concentration. The city of Mecca has many distinctions. It was here that in obedience to God's will, a loved one of Allah—Abraham^{as}—left his wife and child without

Concentrating in Prayers

any provisions and protection. Since he did it for the sake of God, He multiplied his progeny, which is innumerable like the stars in the sky. Many prophets were born in his progeny. Finally, the person destined to reform the whole mankind was also raised from his progeny.

When someone realizes the wisdom of turning his face towards Mecca, he is inspired by the sacrifice of Hadhrat Ishmael[as]. His mind is drawn to the fact that God, for Whose worship he is now standing, is the Lord of Great Honor and Majesty. This realization helps eliminate stray thoughts and leads one to the recognition of the Grandeur and Glory of Allah.

4. Calling of *Adhan* (call to Prayer) also helps in concentration. The call of "*AllahoAkbar AllahoAkbar*" (Allah is the Greatest, Allah is the Greatest) reminds worshippers that God, to Whose presence they are being summoned, is the Greatest. This will promote concentration in their Prayer. The Holy Prophet[saw] says that the *Adhan* is called to put Satan to flight.

When someone realizes that the objective of *Adhan* is to express the Grandeur and Glory of God, he will appreciate its wisdom. Having learned about this philosophy, you will now remember it when you hear the *Adhan* and will receive its full benefit. When the remembrance of the Greatness and Glory of God takes hold of your mind, other thoughts will vanish and concentration will be achieved.

5. *Iqamat* (the shorter version of *Adhan* recited at the beginning of *Salat* in congregation) also draws attention to the Greatness and Glory of God. All the points made concerning *Adhan* apply to it too. The Holy Prophet[saw] says that *Iqamat*, too, puts Satan to flight. He meant that *Iqamat* removes evil inclination and promotes concentration in worship.

6. Order in outwardly arrangements creates order in thoughts and does not let them disperse. When the rows are physically formed for Prayer, deeper thoughts are also lined up. And what an awe-inspiring form the rows represent in Prayers—everybody standing before the King of kings in utter silence! The Holy Prophet[saw] says, "Keep your rows straight; lest your hearts become crooked." What

is the significance of the rows? Simply that the external disorder would adversely affect spiritual harmony.

7. The seventh means of achieving concentration in Prayers is *Niyyat* (intention) because when you command your mind to do something it attends to it. *Niyyat* does not mean that you have to verbalize the name of the *Imam*, the numbers of the *Raka'at,* and facing the *Ka'aba*. The intention of offering *Salat* should be made in the heart.

It is said that somebody developed a phobia concerning *Niyyat,* and, in particular, about specifying the *Imam* (one who leads the Prayer). If he stood in a line behind others, saying "Behind this *Imam*" did not satisfy him. He suspected that since there were other people between him and the *Imam,* he was not really behind that *Imam.* So he moved forward and said, "Behind this *Imam.*" Still dissatisfied, he moved further still and touching the *Imam* said, "Behind this *Imam.*" Those who suffer from such superstitions are wrong. They suffer the consequences. The *Niyyat* is turned in to an unnecessary burden.

In truth the intention is related to the heart. When you stand for Prayers, think actively about the Prayers. Remind yourselves what you are about to do. As soon as you understand this, you will begin to develop humbleness and will begin to concentrate.

8. In congregational Prayers the *Imam* repeats words which create the fear of Allah. Anybody who becomes distracted is nudged and reminded. When *AllahoAkbar* is called he is warned: Stand with full attention because the One in Whose presence you are standing is the Greatest. Then, after a while, when thoughts are distracted, the *Imam* again makes the same reminder. Again, after a while, he is told: *Sami-Allaho li man Hamida* (God listens to him who praises Him)—reminding him that in order to benefit from the Prayer, he must spend the time in praising Allah; otherwise, he is wasting his time.

Repeated reminders from the *Imam* make the followers alert and attentive. This is why the *Imam* has a rank ahead of the followers; he reminds them again and again that they are standing in the presence of the Greatest of all Kings and, therefore, must stand with full attention.

Concentrating in Prayers

9. Islam has not adopted a single posture for Prayers but different positions. If someone gets absorbed in other thoughts, his going in *Ruku* (bowing), *Sajdah* (prostration) reminds him. Even if someone moves to these postures as a habit, the simple act of making the movements makes the mind alert. Worship in other religions does not posses this characteristic; it is unique to Islam.

10. Performance of *Sunnah* before and after obligatory Prayers also helps achieve concentration, especially during the obligatory Prayers.

It is a law of nature that signs of coming events start appearing before their occurrence and the after-effects continue after they have occurred. For example, light spreads before the sun appears in the morning and continues after it sets in the evening. We also observe that some worries dominate the mind at the cost of other thoughts. Matters which accord with one's wishes, or those resulting in pleasure, or those whose absence can be harmful, overpower other matters and preoccupy the mind.

If someone is engaged in a task which does not appear very beneficial to him, and if he has to perform something which is likely to benefit him or can harm him if not done, or is of special interest to him, his thoughts would be absorbed in the second task even when he is doing the first. Take, for example, a worker in an office. If he has to carry out a personal task after office hours, he will start thinking about it an hour or two before he leaves his office. Conversely, if he is engaged in an important assignment in the office, he will continue thinking about it when he leaves his office. Only after some time will he be able to concentrate fully on his other tasks.

The Holy Prophet[saw] has prescribed *Sunnahs* before and after the *Fard* Prayers to make sure that the *Fard* are not vitiated by wandering thoughts. Such distractions are suppressed during the performance of *Sunnahs* and make a man fully prepared and attentive during the performance of *Fard* Prayers. Similarly, *Sunnah* have been appointed after the *Fard* Prayers, to stop the thoughts of pending business from vitiating the last part of the *Fard* Prayers. Thus, the whole of the *Fard* Prayer is protected. As I stated, stray thoughts generally arise when an earlier task is about to be completed and the mind is being prepared for the second. If one believes at the end of his *Fard* Prayers that he has not yet finished—the *Sunnahs* still remain—his thoughts will remain suppressed. This is one of the major reasons for the appointment of *Sunnahs*.

Concentrating in Prayers

The Holy Prophet^{saw} has appointed the number of *Sunnahs* in accordance with the requirements of the time.

The time of *Zuhr* Prayer (early afternoon) is the time of great involvement in other tasks. He has therefore appointed two or four *Sunnahs* before and after the *Fard*. He has appointed two sentries to safeguard the *Fard* from any wandering thoughts.

There are no *Sunnahs* before *Asr* (late Afternoon Prayer) but there are *Nawafil*—one may observe them or skip them—because it is time to finish off business activities. The Prayer for this time is therefore very brief. But there is *Zikr* between *Asr* and *Maghrib* (evening) Prayers.

There are no *Sunnahs* before *Maghrib* Prayer because the time is generally very short; but there are *Sunnahs* after *Maghrib*. Dinner is generally taken after *Maghrib*. The two *Sunnahs* safeguard the mind from being absorbed in thoughts about food or other similar affairs.

There are no *Sunnahs* before *Isha* Prayer because the kinds of activity before *Isha* do not absorb one's mind for long; but there are *Sunnahs* and *Vitr* after *Isha* which protect the mind from the thoughts of sleep. The *Vitr* can also be performed later.

There are two *Sunnahs* before *Fajr* (Morning Prayer); they serve to get rid of the slumber. There are no *Sunnahs* after *Fajr* because generally there is not much activity to preoccupy one's mind after *Fajr*. But *Zikr* has been prescribed between *Fajr* and sunrise.

All of the above methods of maintaining concentration in Prayer have been prescribed in the *Shari'ah*. You can benefit from them fully if you understand their philosophy and keep reminding yourselves of their wisdom. I have described these methods in detail to enable you to understand them fully. God willing, those who act upon them, giving due regard to their philosophy, will derive great benefit.

It should also be remembered that just as the human body has joints, so do the Prayers. The joints of the Prayers consist of words which are recited during standing, bowing, and prostrating postures. Pay special attention to these joints to make your Prayer very strong and upright; otherwise, it will fall.

Other Methods of Maintaining Concentration

Concentrating in Prayers

I will turn to methods which are not the required conditions of Prayer, nor has the *Shari'ah* prescribed them as components of Prayer, but which can help maintain concentration in Prayer.

11. If you are unable to concentrate, recite the words slowly. The human brain instantly recalls things which it has observed often, but it has difficulty in recalling things which it has rarely observed. If you see Tom everyday you will visualize him immediately when you think of him, but if you see him occasionally, his image will appear only after a little while—and that, too, not very clearly. Similarly, if you learn a language in childhood, images are formed immediately when words are uttered. When the words for water and bread are spoken, they quickly bring to mind real things which they represent. This is not the case with foreign languages. The mind visualizes the image after some time. When children learn English, and speak a word (like cat), it will seem to be no more than a word to them. But when the corresponding word is spoken in their own vernacular, their mind immediately forms the picture (of a cat).

Many non-Arab Muslims not familiar with Arabic cannot fully concentrate in Prayers. Concentration requires that the meanings of the words be stored in their minds. Without it, they cannot recall the images instantaneously. They may be saying the fourth verse of *Surah Al-Fatiha*, *Iyyaka Na'abodo* (Thee alone do we worship), while their mind is still in the process of recalling the image of the second verse, *Al-Rahman ir Raheem* (the Gracious, the Merciful). Hence, their concentration is affected and the benefit of the Prayer is reduced.

It is essential for those with poor command of Arabic to recite the words slowly. Until their mind forms a good picture of one phrase, they should not proceed to the next. They should say *"Bismillah ir Rahman ir Raheem"* (In the name of Allah, Most Gracious Ever Merciful) and try to form a good image of its true significance. They should not proceed to *"Alhamdolillah Rabbil-Aalameen"* (All Praise belongs to Allah, Lord of all the worlds) until the image of the previous phrase is vivid and clear. The same applies to the next phrase—*"Maliki Yaumiddin"* (Master of the Day of Judgement). Unless they get into the habit of such slow and deliberate recitation, the words on their lips would be different from the images in their minds.

Concentrating in Prayers

Even those who understand Arabic will benefit from slow recitation. Although they will be able to recall the images quickly, hurried recitation will not allow time for the absorption of corresponding feelings in their hearts. They should also recite the Holy Qur'an slowly and punctuate it with frequent pauses.

Slow recitation is a good habit not only in the reading of the Holy Qur'an but also in general when giving or receiving advice and admonitions. Once Hadhrat Abu Hurairah[ra], was narrating a Hadith quickly and loudly. Hadhrat A'isha[ra] asked who it was and what was he doing. He told his name and added that he was narrating a saying of the Holy Prophet[saw]. She asked, "Is this the manner in which the Holy Prophet[saw], used to hold his discussions?" He had no reply.

The way of the Holy Prophet[saw] is to use a deliberate manner not only in recitation but also in general conversation. Follow his way. It will eliminate the confusion between the words you speak and the images formed in your minds. It is an excellent way of maintaining concentration.

12. The twelfth method has been enjoined by the Holy Prophet[saw]. He has instructed that the eyes must be focused on the place of prostration during Prayers. Many people ignore this instruction. They close their eyes during Prayers, thinking that they would thereby achieve concentration. Not so. Concentration can only be achieved by keeping the eyes open. That is why the Holy Prophet[saw] has advised us to keep our eyes open. In his book *Awariful Ma'arif,* Hadhrat Shahabuddin Suherwardi says that during *Ruku* the eyes should be focused upon the space between the two feet. I agree with this suggestion; it is beneficial for the eyes and creates humility.

There is great wisdom in fixing the sight at one point. It is a characteristic of human nature that when one of the senses is totally preoccupied the other senses become disengaged. When the eyes concentrate fully, the faculty of hearing will not work. If someone calls you at that time you will not hear his voice. Similarly, when the ears are preoccupied, the sense of smell will not function. But if none of the senses is preoccupied, different types of wandering thoughts will flood into the mind. If the eyes are totally preoccupied during Prayer the mind will no longer wander.

Concentrating in Prayers

This phenomenon has now been proven with experiments in physiology., but just think that the Holy Prophet[saw] gave the instructions to keep the eyes open and fixed upon the place of prostration fourteen hundred years ago, at a time when such scientific discoveries had not been made. Moreover, he identified the sense which must be totally preoccupied to save man from wandering thoughts.

Senses of smell and hearing cannot achieve this objective because their action is often involuntary. Employing the sense of smell to achieve this objective requires that arrangement be made to obtain different types of perfumes. If people with different scents pass by, attention would be diverted. The same is the case with the sense of hearing. Nobody can control what he wants to hear and what he does not. If several sounds arise simultaneously, one is bound to hear them all. Indeed, in that case none may be clearly heard. Thus, if you employ the sense of hearing, the ears will either hear all the sounds or none at all.

In contrast to the senses of hearing and smelling, the sight can be controlled. A man can turn his eyes away from what he does not want to see and can focus his attention on what he wants to see. Under the commandment of God, the Holy Prophet[saw] selected the sense of sight for achieving concentration in Prayer.

The Holy Prophet[saw] has also directed that the place of prostration should be free from decoration and should be uniformly simple. When a Muslim focuses his sight upon the place of prostration the results will be very beneficial. His thoughts will concentrate upon worship by the continuous reminder of the prostration. His other senses—which as a rule can either be active or suppressed—will be totally suppressed. Since thoughts are prompted by external influences, which in turn are perceived through the senses, the fact that eyes have been put to work and the other senses are not fully operational will enable the person to concentrate on his Prayer.

Once, a decorated sheet was placed where the Holy Prophet[saw] offered his Prayer. He ordered it to be removed; pointing out that it affects concentration in Prayer. His instruction was for the benefit of his followers.

13. As I mentioned earlier, *Niyyat* (the intention) is required at the beginning of Prayer. It will also be helpful if, at the beginning of the Prayer, you resolve not to let any stray thoughts distract your

mind. Everybody knows that such thoughts are undesirable. But people are prone to forget and a reminder at the beginning of each Prayer would surely help.

Concentrating in Prayers

14. When following an *Imam*, the recitations made by the *Imam* will keep you awake and alert. The *Imam* thus protects his followers. This, incidentally, shows how important it is to offer Prayer behind an *Imam*. When offering Prayer alone, you should follow an excellent method applied by the Holy Prophet[saw], his Companions, and many pious Muslims. Some verses of the Holy Qur'an are particularly conducive of humbleness; repeat them often. For instance, when reciting *Surah Al-Fatiha*, repeat the following verse often:

$$\text{اِيَّاكَ نَعْبُدُ وَاِيَّاكَ نَسْتَعِيْنُ} *$$

Thee alone do we worship and Thee alone we implore for help. (1:5)

This would put the soul to remorse. If it is lost in random thoughts, the soul will return to the act of worship feeling that since it is claiming to worship God alone, it should not wander around.

15. The next method is to help those who cannot hold their concentration for long. Like infants unable to bear hunger or to hold food for long, they need frequent support. A useful technique for them is to concentrate on one posture at a time. When they stand for *Qiyam* they should resolve not to let any thoughts disturb them up to the end of *Ruku*. Going in to *Ruku* they should make the same resolution for the time up to the end of *Ruku*. They should do the same at every change of posture. This will give them great strength to over power any distracting thoughts.

16. If you succumb to other worldly thoughts, they will chase you. But if you confront your thoughts and resolve not to let them disturb you, they will stop. Offer a stiff resistance, therefore, to all such thoughts; stop them immediately. For example, if during the Prayer, you think of your sick child, stop thinking of it by telling yourself that the child is not going to get better by thinking about him nor is he going to get worse if you do not think of him. Resolve, therefore, not to think of him. Continue this practice about every thought until you get a masterly command over them.

Concentrating in Prayers

17. When you offer *Nawafil* at home, recite the words loud enough to hear them. Since the ears are not plugged; they continue to be partly functional. When you hear the words, your mind will be more inclined towards remembrance of God. This method should generally be practiced during the night. If you put the ears to use in Prayers during the day, they will be distracted by all kinds of noise.

18. Fresh thoughts arise from new movements. The movements made during Prayer are a part of the worship and, therefore, they do not give rise to extraneous thoughts. But if other movements are made, they will distract you from the Prayer. The Holy Prophet[saw] has instructed that no unnecessary movement should be made during Prayer.

Movement does indeed disperse thoughts. If someone accidentally touches his coat he may start thinking that the coat is very old and he needs a new one. Then he may start wondering where he will find the money. Then he may get absorbed in how meager his salary is, or how delayed the last payment was, or—if he received it late due to the negligence of an officer—how bad his officer is. Then he may get lost into thoughts of how he is going to get even with his officer. Still absorbed in this chain of thoughts, he will hear the *Imam* say "*Assalamo Alaikum wa Rahmatullah*" and he will finish his Prayer without having performed any real worship.

The Holy Prophet[saw] has forbidden all types of extraneous movements during Prayer. Even if there are pebbles at the place of prostration, they should not be removed unless they cause unbearable pain—and that only once. In brief, all types of motion unrelated to Prayer should be avoided.

19. Perform *Qiyam, Ruku,* and *Sajdah* with alertness. When standing for *Qiyam* do not put all of the weight on one leg leaving the other leg hanging loose. When you are slack yourself, the enemy can overpower you. Physical slackness leads to spiritual slackness.

20. The next method has been used to excess by some *Sufis*.. I do not like to carry things to excess. Nonetheless I will mention it. Used in moderation, it can be beneficial.

Hadhrat Junaid of Baghdad was a holy man of great standing. One of his followers was Shibli, a sincere and righteous man. Shibli used to be the governor of a province. Once, when he was present in the court of the king, a tribal chief received a royal mantle in recognition of his services. The chief was suffering from cold. It so happened that right at the time when he was standing before the king, his nose started flowing. The chief had no handkerchief. When he thought the king was not looking, the chief wiped his nose with the royal robe. The king noticed it and was very angry; he felt that the royal dress had been disgraced. Shibli—who had fear of God in his heart—was so shocked by this incident that he fell unconscious. When he regained consciousness, he resigned from governorship. When asked, Shibli told the king, "You gave a dress to a chief, and become so furious when he disgraced it. I have been granted so many blessings by God. How great will be his punishment if I do not thank Him."

Concentrating in Prayers

Then he went to Hadhrat Junaid and asked him to be admitted as a pupil. He said, "I cannot accept you as a student; you have been a governor and in that capacity you have been cruel to so many people." Shibli pleaded, "Is there anything I can do?" Junaid advised him to go to every house in his area to apologize and offer compensation for the wrongs he had committed. He did accordingly.

The accounts of Shibli's life record that whenever he noticed any slackness or distracting thoughts while offering *Nawafil* he used to beat himself with a stick, till the stick would break. Then he would start again. In the beginning he used to keep a bundle of sticks with him. What he did was excessive and I believe that Islam does not permit carrying things to such extremes. However, since the matter is related entirely to his own self I cannot hold him to criticism.

There is a way of disciplining the self, which is not excessive. Whenever your thoughts are distracted, identify the portion which you were reciting when the thoughts started floating away. Then continue reciting that portion. The self will then realize that you are determined in your worship of God. This realization will eliminate further confusion in thoughts and you will achieve peace and concentration.

21. There is another great and useful technique. A characteristic of true believers is that:

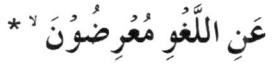

They shun all that is vain. (23:4)

Concentrating in Prayers

Those who are in the habit of entertaining vain and frivolous thoughts will be subjected to similar thoughts during Prayer. If they train themselves not to think of such thoughts at all, they will be saved from the distraction of thoughts during Prayer too. There are many who indulge in fables like the proverbial Sheikh Chilli of Iran. Such thoughts do them no good. The mind should not be permitted to indulge in thoughts which are conjectural and superficial. There is, of course, no harm in thinking of useful and beneficial things. Particularly useless are thoughts of past things which cannot be changed. To worry about such things is indeed the height of foolishness.

It should be obvious that human efforts focus towards whatever they are directed. If someone turns his mind towards futile thoughts, he loses the ability to focus on the useful. Therefore, stop your frivolous thoughts and turn your attention to beneficial ideas. If you do that, your mind will get into the habit of deliberating on the beneficial ideas. To think of other things while performing one task is frivolous except in some cases. The mind of a person who has trained it to focus on the useful will not think of other things during Prayer.

22. The next technique is very useful; it takes spirituality to its zenith. The Holy Prophet[saw] was once asked, "What is *Ihsan* (goodness)?" He responded, *"Pray to Allah as if you are seeing Him; but as a minimum be aware that He is seeing you."*

When you stand for Prayer imagine that you are standing in the presence of God and you can see Him—not in His physical form but in His Glory and Greatness. This creates a fear of greatness and power of God in the mind. The mind becomes careful not to do anything untoward at that time. If you cannot visualize God, believe, as a minimum, that He is watching you. He is fully aware of everything you are doing. Think hard. When you say *Alhamdolillah* (All Praise belongs to Allah) does the condition of your heart affirm that spirit? Or is it engaged in some other thoughts altogether? If the mind is engaged in different directions, warn yourself and make your heart join what is being uttered by the tongue.

The Holy Prophet[saw] says that any servant of God who offers two *Raka'at* with such devotion that he does not indulge in any kind of communication with the self is freed from all his sins. Imagine, then, the status of one who always remains in that state. To concentrate fully towards God during Prayer is therefore not an ordinary matter.

The methods, which I have described to you, with the Grace of God, should not be treated lightly. Act on them sincerely. If you do, you will be greatly blessed.

Concentrating in Prayers

At the conclusion of the Prayer, we say the familiar Islamic greeting of *"Assalamo Alaikum wa Rahmatullah"*. This is a wonderful indicator for maintaining concentration. You say *"Assalamo Alaikum..."* when you come from somewhere. When a Muslim says *"Assalamo Alaikum wa Rahmatullah"* at the conclusion of his Prayer, he is stating that he had gone to express his obedience and servitude to God and has now returned. He is saying that he is bringing the message of peace and blessings for his fellow Muslims. Since he was always physically present at that place, the only meaning can be that his spirit was prostrating in the presence of God—he was so busy in the worship that he was cut off and absent from the world. Saying *"Assalamo Alaikum..."* at the conclusion of Prayer indicates that it is essential for a Muslim to be alert in safeguarding his Prayer, because he is, at that time, present in the court of God Almighty, Who says about Muslims that:

...وَهُمْ عَلٰى صَلَا تِهِمْ يُحَا فِظُوْنَ*

...and they keep a watch over their Prayer. (6:93)

Satan wants to disrupt their Prayers but vigilant Muslims safeguard their Prayers from his attacks.

Everybody should, therefore, guard his Prayers. When you offer Prayer, keep in mind that you have entered in the presence of God. When you return you should give glad tidings to those to the right and those to the left that you have brought peace and blessings for them. But if someone has never gone to God's presence, and has always remained engrossed in his own thoughts, he will be telling a big lie when he says *"Assalamo Alaikum wa Rahmatullah."* He is trying to tell people that he is returning from God, whereas he never went there.

Make every effort to safeguard your Prayers. Put up a strong resistance to Satan for he is trying to keep you away from God. Remember that even if your entire Prayer is spent in a constant struggle and you do not yield to Satan, Allah will consider you present in His audience. But if you yield, He will let you go. Continue your struggle; you will succeed in the end.

Public Proclamation as Remembrance

I have so far mentioned three types of *Zikr*—prescribed Prayers, recitation of the Holy Qur'an and remembrance of Allah other than Prayer, done privately. One type of *Zikr*, which is done publicly, yet remains. It is performed in to two ways:

1. When we meet fellow Muslims, we should talk about Allah's Power and Glory and recall His Blessings, instead of indulging in frivolous and vain talk. This purifies the heart and a beneficent impression is made on the innermost feelings.

Once, the Holy Prophet[saw] came out of his house. He saw some people engaged in Prayer in the Mosque. Some others were sitting in a circle talking of faith. He joined the latter group and said, "*What these people are doing is better.*" This shows that public proclamation is sometimes superior to remembrance in private.

There are times when remembrance in private is essential. But when many people are present it is more beneficial to recite publicly to share the spiritual experiences with each other. Keeping to oneself under these circumstances may lead to pretence. Exposition of the meanings of the Holy Qur'an is also included in this type of *Zikr*. Similarly, inviting fellow Muslims to acts of goodness is counted as *Zikr*.

2. Then there is *Zikr* done in the meeting of the opponents. All religions other than Islam are guilty of acts of omission or commission in describing the attributes of God. To nonetheless describe the true status and Glory of God in their meetings is therefore a form of *Zikr*. Allah says:

يَآ يُّهَا الْمُدَّثِّرُ ۟ ٭ قُمْ فَاَنْذِرْ ۟ ٭ وَرَبَّکَ فَكَبِّرْ ۟ ٭

O thou that has wrapped thyself with thy mantle. Arise and warn and thy Lord do thou magnify... (74:2–4)

Benefits of Zikr

To warn people and to express the Greatness of God before them has been included here as *Takbeer* which is a part of *Zikr*.

To conclude, expressing the attributes of Allah to the people belonging to other faiths is *Zikr*. Chapter 87 of the Holy Qur'an, (*Surah Al-Ala*) also points to the same fact. The word *Zikr* has been used specifically for such activities in *Surah Al-Ala*, which says:

$$فَذَكِّرْ اِنْ نَّفَعَتِ الذِّكْرٰى$$

So go on reminding; surely, reminding is profitable. (87:10)

Benefits of Zikr

I will now turn to the benefits of *Zikr*.

1. The greatest benefit of *Zikr* is that it leads to the pleasure of God—not just like any other good deed, but in a special way.

The reward of a deed is commensurate with its importance. God Almighty says about *Zikr* that it is the greatest of all affairs. At another place in the Holy Qur'an, He says:

$$وَعَدَاللّٰهُ الْمُؤْمِنِيْنَ وَالْمُؤْمِنٰتِ جَنّٰتٍ تَجْرِىْ مِنْ تَحْتِهَا الْاَنْهٰرُ خٰلِدِيْنَ فِيْهَا وَمَسٰكِنَ طَيِّبَةً فِىْ جَنّٰتِ عَدْنٍ ۚ وَرِضْوَانٌ مِّنَ اللّٰهِ اَكْبَرُ ۚ ذٰلِكَ هُوَ الْفَوْزُ الْعَظِيْمُ$$

Allah has promised to the believers, Men and women, Gardens beneath which rivers flow, wherein they will abide, and delightful dwelling-places in Gardens of Eternity. And the pleasure of Allah is greatest of all, that is the supreme triumph. (9:72)

The greatest reward is the pleasure of Allah. The greatest of all rewards can only result from the greatest of deeds, which is *Zikr*. Hence the reward of *Zikr* is the pleasure of Allah. In the above verse God Almighty distinguishes the pleasure of Allah from other rewards. This shows that it is something different, and is the greatest of all. Indeed, for a true believer there can be no reward higher than receiving the pleasure of his Lord.

Allah has clearly indicated that if you carry out *Zikr-i-Ilahi,* the greatest of all deeds, you will receive the pleasure of Allah, the greatest of all rewards.

Benefits of Zikr

2. Remembrance of Allah can lead to the comfort and peace of the heart. Allah says:

$$اَلَّذِيْنَ اٰمَنُوْا وَ تَطْمَئِنُّ قُلُوْبُهُمْ بِذِكْرِ اللّٰهِ ۗ اَلَا بِذِكْرِ اللّٰهِ تَطْمَئِنُّ الْقُلُوْبُ ۚ*$$

Those who believe and whose hearts find comfort in the remembrance of Allah. Aye! It is in the remembrance of Allah that hearts can find comfort. (13:29)

Hearts find comfort in *Zikr*. Why? Because anxiety is caused by the fear of an impending calamity. If a man believes that there is a remedy for every ailment, he will not be worried. When someone remembers Allah and realizes that with His unlimited powers, He can remove all types of difficulties; his heart comforts him by saying, "Why do I need to be concerned? I have an All-Powerful God; He will surely remove my troubles." Such thoughts provide peace of mind.

3. Allah befriends him who spends his time in His remembrance. He provides him a place in His audience even when he is still in this world. As He says:

$$فَاذْكُرُوْنِيْ اَذْكُرْكُمْ وَاشْكُرُوْلِيْ وَ لَا تَكْفُرُوْنِ*$$

Therefore remember Me, and I will remember you; and be thankful to Me and do not be ungrateful to Me. (2:153)

Just as the worldly kings invite people to their royal audience when they are pleased with them, so does Allah.

4. Remembrance of Allah saves one from sins. God Almighty says in the Holy Qur'an:

$$اُتْلُ مَآ اُوْحِيَ اِلَيْكَ مِنَ الْكِتٰبِ وَاَقِمِ الصَّلٰوةَ ۗ اِنَّ الصَّلٰوةَ تَنْهٰى عَنِ الْفَحْشَآءِ وَالْمُنْكَرِ ۗ وَلَذِكْرُ اللّٰهِ اَكْبَرُ وَاللّٰهُ يَعْلَمُ مَا تَصْنَعُوْنَ*$$

Benefits of Zikr

Recite that which has been revealed to thee of the book, and observe Prayer. The Prayer surely restrains one from indecency and manifest evil, and remembrance of Allah indeed is the greatest virtue. And Allah knows what you do. (29:46)

Prayer saves you from indecency and evil. As I stated earlier, Prayer is a form of remembrance of Allah. Hence remembrance of Allah guards against sins. *Zikr* is weighty. When it falls upon the head of Satan, he will be crushed to death and will no longer incite you towards evil.

5. Remembrance of Allah strengthens the hearts, and promotes the spirit of fighting evil. As God Almighty says:

$$\text{يَا أَيُّهَا الَّذِينَ اٰمَنُوْٓا اِذَا لَقِيتُمْ فِئَةً فَاثْبُتُوْا وَاذْكُرُوا اللّٰهَ كَثِيْرًا لَّعَلَّكُمْ تُفْلِحُوْنَ}$$

O ye who believe! When you encounter an army, remain firm, and remember Allah much that you may prosper. (8:46)

According to this verse the way to encounter a strong enemy is to remember Allah in abundance.

6. A person who remembers Allah will be successful in all his affairs, provided that he remembers Allah with utmost fidelity. This is proven by the verse which I recited earlier. Allah says:

$$\text{وَاذْكُرُوا اللّٰهَ كَثِيْرًا لَّعَلَّكُمْ تُفْلِحُوْنَ}$$

…and remember Allah much that you may prosper. (8:46)

7. The Holy Prophet[saw] says that on the Day of Judgement, seven types of people will be granted the shadow of Allah's Mercy. One of them are the people who remember Allah. The Holy Prophet[saw] adds that it will be a grievous day. Nobody has ever seen the like of it. Allah's wrath will be great that day because all mischief-makers will be presented before Him. The sun will draw near. Anyone who is granted the shadow of Allah's Mercy that day will be lucky indeed!

8. Allah accepts the prayers of those who remember Him. The prayers mentioned in the Holy Qur'an start with *Zikr*, that is, *Tasbeeh* and *Tahmeed*. The first prayer is contained in *Surah Al-Fatiha*. It starts with verses consisting exclusively of *Zikr*.

Benefits of Zikr

بِسْمِ اللّٰهِ الرَّحْمٰنِ الرَّحِيْمِ * اَلْحَمْدُ لِلّٰهِ رَبِّ الْعٰلَمِيْنَ *
الرَّحْمٰنِ الرَّحِيْمِ * مٰلِكِ يَوْمِ الدِّيْنِ *

In the name of Allah, the Most Gracious, Ever Merciful. All Praise belongs to Allah, Lord of all the worlds, The Most Gracious, Ever Merciful, Master of the Day of Judgement. (1:1–4)

Then comes the part, which is partly for God and partly for man:

اِيَّاكَ نَعْبُدُ وَاِيَّاكَ نَسْتَعِيْنُ *

Thee alone do we worship and Thee alone we implore for help. (1:5)

In the end comes the supplication:

اِهْدِنَا الصِّرَاطَ الْمُسْتَقِيْمَ * صِرَاطَ الَّذِيْنَ اَنْعَمْتَ
عَلَيْهِمْ * غَيْرِ الْمَغْضُوْبِ عَلَيْهِمْ وَ لَا الضَّآلِّيْنَ *

Guide us in the right path—the path of those on whom Thou hast bestowed Thy Blessings, and not of those who have incurred Thy displeasure, nor of those who have gone astray. (1:6–7)

Surah Al-Fatiha is a prayer; but God Almighty starts it with remembrance and ends it with the supplication. We observe the same phenomenon in the world. When a beggar comes, he first praises the master of the house and then submits his plea.

Similarly, when a man goes to beg of Allah he should first acknowledge the authority of God and admit his own weakness. Prophet Jonah[as] did the same when he cried in the depth of darkness saying that:

... لَآ اِلٰهَ اِلَّآ اَنْتَ سُبْحٰنَكَ اِنِّيْ كُنْتُ مِنَ الظّٰلِمِيْنَ *

...there is no God but Thou, Holy art Thou. I have indeed been of the wrongdoers. (21:88)

Benefits of Zikr

He first expressed the glory of God, and then he stated the condition in which he found himself. Moreover the Holy Prophet[saw] attributes the following statement to Allah: "He who remains busy in My remembrance receives more from Me than those who merely keep asking." This Hadith does not mean that you should not pray to God. *Surah Al-Fatiha*, which is the Mother of the Book, combines *Zikr* with prayer. Both the Holy Qur'an and the Hadith teach us many prayers. The Hadith only means that one who does not perform *Zikr* but only submits pleas and requests receives less than the one who keeps praying for what he needs and additionally takes the time to perform *Zikr*.

9. *Zikr* is a means of receiving Allah's forgiveness from sins. The Holy Prophet[saw] says that a person who performs *Takbeer*, *Tahmeed*, and *Tasbeeh* is forgiven all his sins even if the sins are innumerable like foam in the sea.

10. *Zikr* sharpens the insight. One who remembers Allah discovers verities and points of wisdom with which he himself is surprised. God Almighty says:

$$\text{اِنَّ فِیْ خَلْقِ السَّمٰوٰتِ وَالْاَرْضِ وَاخْتِلَافِ الَّیْلِ وَالنَّهَارِ}$$
$$\text{لَاٰیٰتٍ لِّاُولِی الْاَلْبَابِ * الَّذِیْنَ یَذْکُرُوْنَ اللّٰهَ قِیٰمًا وَّقُعُوْدًا}$$
$$\text{وَّعَلٰی جُنُوْبِهِمْ وَیَتَفَکَّرُوْنَ فِیْ خَلْقِ السَّمٰوٰتِ وَالْاَرْضِ ۚ}$$
$$\text{رَبَّنَا مَا خَلَقْتَ هٰذَا بَاطِلًا ۚ سُبْحٰنَکَ فَقِنَا عَذَابَ النَّارِ *}$$

In the creation of heavens and the earth and in the alternation of the night and the day there are indeed signs for men of understanding; those who remember Allah while standing, sitting, and lying on their sides, and ponder over the creation of the Heavens and the earth: Our Lord thou hast not created this in vain; Holy art Thou; save us, then, from the punishment of the Fire'. (3:191–192)

11. Remembrance of Allah leads to righteousness. There is a Hadith in which the Holy Prophet[saw] attributes the following statement to God Almighty: When a servant of mine remembers Me in his heart, I remember him in private and if he remembers Me in public, I remember him in public...

This Hadith shows that when, for example, a man says, "Holy art Thou O Allah," Allah returns this with a blessing, May you also become holy and purified. When Allah says that, purification is surely attained. Similarly when a man glorifies the name of Allah among others, Allah raises his good name among people. The world acknowledges him as a righteous man.

It is human nature that if you associate with someone often, your love and affection for them increases. People even begin to love the village or city in which they live. When someone remembers Allah day and night and mentions His name, his love for Allah will gradually increase.

These, in short, are the benefits of remembrance of Allah. I pray that Allah may make them beneficial for me and for all of you. Amen.

Benefits of Zikr

References to the Holy Qur'an

VERSE	PAGE
1:1	23
1:1–4	59
1:2	23, 31
1:5	49, 59
1:6–7	59
2:240	18
2:153	57
2:157	23
3:191–192	60
4:104	19, 24, 30
6:93	53
7:32	39
8:3	15
8:46	58
9:72	56
12:88	17
13:29	57
15:10	19
19:59	15
20:15	18
20:131	30
21:51	19
21:88	59
23:4	51
24:38	19, 20
29:46	3, 57, 58
32:17	37
33:42–43	4
39:24	15
63:10	4
73:7	33, 34
74:2–8	20
74:2–4	55
76:26	3, 30
87:10	56

Index

Adhan
as help in concentration in Prayers 41
defined VII
objective of 42
Ahmadiyya Muslim Community
defined VII
need for Zikr in 5
Allah the Exalted
defined VII
Attributes of
Aleem VII
as Zikr-i-Ilahi 18
blessings of reciting 5
Khabeer VIII
Khaliq VIII
Qadir IX
Quddoos IX
Angels
attracted to gatherings of Zikr 3
existence of 4
Annual Conference
defined VII

Dancing
not a characteristic of
true Zikr-i-Ilahi 16
Du'aa
defined VIII

Fard
defined IX
obligation prescribed by God 33

safeguarding of

Hadhrat
defined VII
Hadhur
defined VII
Hadith
about pillars of Islam 7
against doing Zikr aloud 13
defined VII
on blessings of Zikr 3
on getting up for Tahajjud 35
on the importance of Nawafil 6
reciting slowly 47
Holy Prophet[saw]
defined VIII
on fluctuation being essential in
Zikr 29
on importance of keeping the rows
straight in Prayers 42
on importance of Tahajjud 34
on importance of Zikr 4
on keeping the fast 27
on objective of Adhan 42
on prohibition of doing Zikr aloud 13
on prohibition of exceeding the limits
in Zikr 27
on recitation of Holy Qur'an 27
on reciting Zikr slowly 47
on reserving a place for worship at
homes 41
on unnecessary movement during
Prayer 50

Holy Qur'an
    as Zikr-i-Ilahi 18, 19
    defined VII
    on getting up for Tahajjud 35
    reciting slowly 47
    recitation of 21, 27
Humility
    a characteristics of true Zikr 15

Iqamat
    and help in concentration in Prayer 42

Junaid of Baghdad 50

Ka'aba
    reasons for commandments to face towards 41
Khalifa
    defined VIII
Khalifatul-Masih I
    and performance of Zikr 31
    relationship between cleanliness and purity 38

Mesmerism
    contrasted with Zikr 11
Musleh Mau'ood
    defined VIII

Nawafil
    defined IX
    means of achieving nearness of Allah 6
    philosophy of prescribing 33
Niyyat
    and help in concentration in Prayer 43
    superstition about 43

Pillars of Islam
    Hadith about 7
Poetry
    as Zikr-i-Ilahi? 13
Prayer(s)
    as Zikr-i-Ilahi 33
    concentrating in 40
    congregational at mosque 41
    defined VIII
    different Sunnahs prescribed in 45
    proper observing of 7
    reciting slowly 46
Promised Messiah[as]
    critiques of innovations introduced into Zikr 9
    defined IX

Qa'adah
    defined VIII
Qiyam
    defined VIII

Rak'a
    defined VIII
Remembrance of Allah
    see Zikr-i-Ilahi
Ruku
    defined VIII

Sajdah
    defined VIII
Salat
    as remembrance of Allah 6
    defined VIII
Shibli 50
Sufi(s)
    innovation introduced by 9

Sunnah(s)
   and concentration in Prayers 44
   defined IX
   in different Prayers 44
   numbers of 45
   philosophy of prescribing 33
   protecting the Fards 44

Tahajjud
   alarm clock not preferred 34
   defined IX
   how to get up for 34
   importance of 34
   may sprinkle water to awaken spouse 34

Tahmeed
   and forgiveness of sins 60
   before going to sleep 36
   defined IX, 22
   in Holy Qur'an 59
   on receiving happy news 24

Takbeer
   and forgiveness of sins 60
   defined IX, 22
   part of Zikr 56

Tasbeeh
   and forgiveness of sins 60
   before going to sleep 36
   defined IX, 22
   in Holy Qur'an 56

Tirmidhi
   defined IX

Unconsciousness
   not a characteristics of true Zikr 16

Wudu
   and concentration in Prayers 40

Zakat
   defined IX

Zikr
   See Zikr-I-Ilahi

Zikr-i-Ilahi
   achieving concentration 28
   attributes of Allah as 18
   benefits of 56
   defined IX, 1
   fluctuation is essential 29
   four kinds of 18
   Holy Qur'an as 18, 19
   importance of 1, 3
   methods of performing 21
   Misguided forms of 9
   misunderstandings about 9
   need for 3
   need in Ahmadiyya Community 5
   pleasure from 11
   poetry as? 13
   Prayers as 33
   precautions about 27
   Promised Messiah[as] on 9
   proper times for 27, 30
   public proclamation as 55
   rules out dancing and shouting 16
   Salat as 5
   true characteristics of 15
   unconsciousness not a part of 16
   vs. influence of thoughts 12
   vs. mesmerism 11
   vs. songs and music 13
   with humbleness and fear of Allah 28